2/18

2 9 JUN 2018

Suffolk Libraries

Please return/renew this item
by the last date shown.

Suffolk Libraries
01473 351249
www.suffolklibraries.co.uk

Mother Anguish

Mother Anguish

a memoir

BASIA BRIGGS

QUARTET

First published in 2017 by Quartet Books Limited
A member of the Namara Group
27 Goodge Street, London, W1T 2LD

A catalogue record for this book
is available from the British Library

ISBN 9780704374492

Typeset by Josh Bryson
Printed and bound in Great Britain by
TJ International Ltd, Padstow, Cornwall

To my children, Adam and Camilla.
I did my best.

Chapter 1

I was the product of a *mésalliance* between the Polish son of a great aristocratic landowning family and my mother, daughter of theatrical folk from Warsaw. The two families agreed that only disaster would ensue from such a union as my parents', yet relatives from both sides gathered stoically for the wedding in Hanover, refusing to ever meet each other again.

I was born nine months later. I was a honeymoon baby.

My parents, Jozef and Camilla, met whilst finishing their education in Germany after the war. My mother attended high school there and my father studied estate management and agriculture at university. He loved the palace, Raba Wyżna, where he had been born and brought up and optimistically imagined that the Communist regime might come to an end so that all our family estates would be returned, restoring him to his rightful sphere where he could flourish. I think my father was brought up to do nothing except be a gentleman, ride a horse magnificently and speak French and German and Italian. Sadly his dream was never to be fulfilled as he was to die of a heart attack, at the ridiculously early age of sixty, before the property was given back to the family.

They were a very attractive couple but my parents' marriage was apparently unhappy from the start and they effectively separated a year after I was born.

Mother's father Klemens had been director of the Warsaw National Opera house, and her mother, my granny Anna, sang in the chorus. Granny got pregnant by her boss aged eighteen and he then reluctantly married her. After the birth of her first

1

child, Klemens swiftly impregnated poor Granny again and she gave birth to my mother in 1938, a mere ten months separating the two. Granny told me her husband was unfaithful and cruel to her for overwhelming him with babies so she ran off with his best friend, a piano player, and got a divorce, which was shockingly unheard of in respectable Catholic and censorious 1930s Poland.

On my father's side, my grandfather Tadeusz had already taken part in World War I and then attended further military school training, obtaining the rank of Brigadier General. He fought in World War II until the defeat of Poland and then escaped to England in 1939 and lived in London.

My grandmother, who had the magnificent name of Wanda Melania de Glowno Godziemba Glowinska, took part in the Warsaw Uprising in September 1944. She was arrested and transported to Ravensbrück concentration camp where she was kept in inhuman conditions until the liberation eight months later.

As all her properties had been confiscated in Poland, she emigrated to England where she was to spend the rest of her life. After a few years the German government paid out compensation to concentration camp victims, so she and my grandfather bought a neglected, ramshackle but beautiful Victorian house called Lawday Place near Farnham in Surrey. We all lived together there in true Polish fashion as an extended family, with various dispossessed aunts and uncles and other friends of my grandparents' and it was there that my childhood memories began.

My earliest memories were of how I loved my mother to distraction. She was the most beautiful, the jolliest, most divine smelling goddess of my childhood. No other child's mum was a patch on mine and she was always surrounded by gentlemen admirers, from urbane hand-kissing Polish men to the cheerful cockney milkman who always had a kind word to say to me. Whenever my mother and I went to the local bakery the owner would give me a little chocolate cake for free as he made misty eyed conversation with my mother. She was always dressed to impress in the most elegant attire and would totter around in strappy stiletto heels, even at the most impractical moments. She wouldn't be caught dead in anything one might deem 'casual' and I was absolutely enchanted by her glamour.

I also discovered very early on that she was quite the silliest woman I had ever met and as a small child I would listen solemnly to the stupid things she said and hope no one else noticed. I have a vivid recollection from around the age of three of observing, with some puzzlement, my mother on her hands and knees tossing and splashing perfume repeatedly under her bed. She said a cat had done its smelly business there and she had to mask the stench. The resulting combination of odours was awful and I pitied her distress and thought she was going about it all wrong.

My love for her grew with protective adoration as I knew she needed to be cared for by me. I was never critical or judgemental; I loved her so much and felt that we would have a unique and wonderful future living together for always. My chief ambition in life was to grow up and have a baby girl so I could call her Camilla to show my mother how much I loved her.

I knew my parents' marriage had not been a happy one as whenever my mother spoke of my father her eyes would glisten with hatred and bewilderingly she would hold up her little finger and with some anger in her tone she would say, 'your father has only got one this size.' It was not until some years later that it dawned on me that she was referring to his penis.

I had no idea what she was talking about then. And besides, I have no memory of my parents ever being in the same room together with me. All I knew was that I wasn't allowed to say to my mother that I liked my father, even though I loved him very much and loved touching the leather elbow patches on his tweed jacket.

He had a very formal and dignified character and was remarkably handsome, always smiling and beautifully dressed. Some said he looked just like Sir Laurence Olivier from the movies but I thought he was even handsomer. He was unfailingly courteous and polite to all and I always remember that on greeting other women he would bow and kiss their hand while they smiled at him flirtatiously. I noticed that all the ladies would hover around him and hang on his every word. He would even kiss his own mother's hand upon coming into whichever room she was in, as that was the traditional way of the old Poles' upbringing.

He was very good natured and always had a kind word and a smile for everyone he encountered. I never ever remember him raising his voice at any time, however naughty I was. Occasionally if he was cross with me his voice would become much quieter and that was much more frightening. He didn't like it if I brought hedgehogs into the house as they were covered in fleas. But that was very rare as I adored him and never wanted to give him any trouble, especially as once he parted a hedgehog's spines and I saw indeed that it was crawling with insects.

I have no idea what he did for a living or if he had a regular job as I was too young. I just know that sometimes he was around and sometimes he wasn't. I think he often worked as a skiing instructor and would depart to Austria with a tour from a travel agency.

When at home he played tennis all the time. We had our own tennis court and on summer days many friends would come and play or just sit around watching and having a picnic on the lawn. When he had time he was very keen that I should learn tennis as well and taught me as much as he could.

I have his passport to this day and it states clearly that it is valid for all countries 'except Poland'. He spoke of Poland with terrible homesickness very often, as did my grandparents and they all yearned to return to their homeland where they said the summers were always hotter and the winters snowier and everything was best. Even the tomatoes tasted better. It would not have surprised me if they had said the bananas were even bendier.

Mother Anguish

I wasn't at all interested as I was more than happy living in glorious Surrey and never listened to tales of Poland.

Lawday Place was surrounded by acres of pine woodland and gorse-covered ground, through which a long, winding drive led to the front circular courtyard. The entrance was imposing and visitors would first ascend its few wide steps before entering a small conservatory with 9-ft high windows on every side which preceded the front door. This conservatory was furnished with wicker armchairs and great, soft cushions so that in the case of inclement weather we could sit and still enjoy looking at the garden. Being an established garden of over a hundred years it was glorious and I often wondered what nice family had lived there before us and why on earth did they sell such a beautiful property.

Looking out from this vantage point there was a 20ft-high bank of rhododendrons to the right in all shades of pink and a border of azaleas planted lower down. There were lawns, a tennis court and a badminton court, beyond which stood four mighty beech trees and also two small ornamental lakes. However, the lakes were largely neglected as my grandparents were busy enough and so the water was full of algae and bulrushes grew near the edge, above which dragonflies hovered. Beyond the tennis court and to the left stood a massive, old cedar tree with spreading low branches. This was my favourite place to sit and I would poke my little fingers into the sticky resin seeping out of the bark and sniff it with delight. Behind that we had a rose garden and further away chickens were kept but the coops were well out of sight. I was occasionally taken to gather eggs from underneath the clucking hens. It was paradise and I ran amok, totally unsupervised and undisciplined and spent my days chasing butterflies and looking for caterpillars and other wildlife. In springtime the horse chestnut trees were a magical sight, the meadow was golden with buttercups and I could turn somersaults with the sheer joy of living.

We also had two horses called Kasia and Kuba. One day Kuba fell into a ditch and the fire brigade was called to haul him out. I remember being told by some uncle to hurry and not miss the dramatic spectacle and I was beside myself with excitement and couldn't eat my breakfast but my mother insisted I eat my egg or not go. I desperately tried to explain how important this once in a lifetime occasion was but she was adamant that I eat my egg. How can you be so silly not to realise that I can eat the egg afterwards, I thought as I watched her putting on her lipstick and fluffing her hair. I think she must have had a date with a man as when I begged her to come and see the horse too, she was not interested at all. So by the time I got to the ditch Kuba was safely out and back in the field.

The house had ten large bedrooms, each one occupied by some aged relative, and I ran amok there too, bothering everyone, though as the only child in the house I was much loved and cosseted and everyone seemed to want a hand in my upbringing. One aunt taught me to bake bread and I was thrilled to see the yeast rising. Another taught me to knit and embroider. There was also a one-legged uncle who sat in a wheelchair all day every day by the window of one of the best bedrooms at the front. He was a depressed man and rarely talked much but he did tell me that his leg, the one which wasn't there, was always itchy or cold. I cannot ever remember being punished, though I was once reprimanded for trying to clean the windows of the conservatory and making a dreadful mess with suds just before guests were expected. The house had three large reception rooms and three staircases too; one gracious main one leading up from the hall, a middle one mysteriously ascending from behind a door to I know not where upstairs, and right at the back of the house there was another staircase obviously built for the servants, although we didn't have any as we weren't rich enough.

In Poland my grandmother Wanda had been the sole owner of an estate of thousands of acres since the age of twelve. She was an only child and her father, my great-grandfather, had committed suicide by shooting himself in the head at the age of thirty-seven. He had had to all appearances an enchanted life; he was a man of vision and constantly kept abreast of the latest in technology from England, using modern tractors and machinery to make his workers operate efficiently. I was told that he was very popular with the working peasantry and busied himself making sure that they had the most comfortable cottages and conditions. He made frequent visits to Harrods in London to buy fishing and hunting equipment. It is a mystery to this day as to why he killed himself.

Grandmother Wanda's estate was confiscated by the Russians but I like to think she experienced some happiness in Surrey. Her husband, my adored grandfather, had been a famous wartime general so both were considered very prominent in England's Polish exile society and it was a great honour to be invited to Lawday Place for a weekend or Sunday afternoon tea. I think to make ends meet in running such a large house she had to resort to charging for a week's visit.

I remember the many guests would always sit around a huge mahogany dining table and if they were scattered around the grounds when it was set for a meal, I was allowed to sound the gong to assemble them. I was allowed to sit at table in the daytime but not for dinners. For evening events I had to satisfy myself with a bird's-eye view through the bannisters at the top of the landing.

The visitors were an assorted bunch of august dignitaries; war pilots with their beautifully dressed wives, though none of them half as pretty as my mother, and other soldiers with various interesting scars and wounds, squashed heads and eye patches. I remember one man who had an artificial arm made of wood and covered in leather and I was much impressed as he could still drive with only one hand. He came to us from London in a red MG roaring up the drive. He was very glamorous.

My grandfather, the patriarch, would sit at the head of the table and the conversation flowed. Whenever they didn't want me to understand what was being said they spoke in French or German. They seemed fluent in all languages except English. On Sundays it was always very jolly as the old military commander would lead us to church, which was a long way away. We all walked single file along country roads and counted the many run-over hedgehogs along the way. My mother was jealous of the affection I had for my grandfather and told me to stop following him around and bothering him as he was a '*staruszek*', being Polish for a very old man. That night, as he was reading me my bedtime story I interrupted and asked him if it was true that he was a *staruszek*. He looked subdued and a bit sad as he would only have been about seventy at the time.

Every morning my grandfather would rush to catch the train to London where he was involved with Polish-government-in-exile issues. He also had an office in Queen's Gate Terrace where he ran a fund to support the widows of the Katyn massacre victims. 22,000 young officers had been murdered by the Russians, each with a single bullet through the head, and then buried in a communal grave in the forest. They left behind very young widows, many of whom lived to an advanced old age and my grandfather was passionate about their welfare.

I was so proud of him and the respect which he was shown by everyone. When he took me one day to the Polish Club for lunch, so many people approached bowing to honour him. Once we were buying a ticket at Gloucester Road Underground station and suddenly the ticket seller called out 'General, General, do you remember me?' With that this unknown man left his seat behind a murky piece of window and dashed around the side to greet my grandfather, falling to his knees and clasping his hand. Apparently he had been an inferior subaltern during the war and was thrilled to see my granddad.

Mother Anguish

Sometimes in the morning he would allow me to watch him shave, which he did with an old-fashioned cut-throat razor. He kept his small beard and moustache but shaved his cheeks and the whole of his head completely bald. This, I was told, was due to an episode during the war when he was on the run and would have been executed if captured, so he altered his appearance and grew hair where there previously was none and shaved off the part where there was. When he found himself in safety his comrades laughed and said the new look suited him so he kept it. In the bathroom he was most particular about cleaning his teeth, which he did with Eucryl Smokers Toothpowder. He never touched a cigarette but it obviously scrubbed them to perfection. Afterwards he would gargle with salty water and then by some miracle he would toss his head back and forward and exhale a great gush of the salty water out through his nose. I tried it once and nearly choked to death but his method was quick and routine and he praised this habit for his excellent health and never catching a cold.

His standard of dignity was inordinately high and he dressed immaculately, changing his stiff shirt collars twice a day. These were delivered weekly from a laundry and I marvelled at the rock-solid stiffness he was quite happy to have around his neck, a very old-fashioned style that he kept to for the rest of his life. His shoes were polished to gleaming perfection and one morning I was naughty and tied his shoelaces on each shoe to the other so that he would miss his train to London and stay home and spend the day with me.

He was a scholarly man, having also been a lawyer in Krakow before the war, and he fired my enthusiasm for learning on many subjects. On a clear, crisp night he would bundle me up with scarves and take me out to point out the stars and teach me about the night sky and the solar system. Another time he woke me to come to the barn to watch a cow giving birth. If I had been a good girl, some nights, as a special treat, my grandmother would

9

allow me to stay up until 10 p.m. and wait for him to come home from London. I used to sit by the window in the one-legged uncle's room on the top floor of the house and stare into the dark distance and soon I would see the light from my grandfather's torch as he made his way through the woodland up the drive.

My grandmother was a kind, calm woman, usually dressed in grey or black with a white little collar. She had a haunted look in her eyes; I don't think the horrors of Ravensbrück ever left her and I know she went for regular electric shock treatment, a standard treatment for depression which she said made her feel better, though it was a barbaric procedure. She had a clear pink complexion, of which she was very proud and she told me she splashed herself with very cold water every night and morning to achieve it. My grandparents were a devoted couple and it amused me how whenever in conversation she had reason to make facial expressions, my grandfather would exclaim with horror using her nickname: 'Dulinka, Dulinka, don't frown your beautiful forehead or you will get wrinkles.' Because she had endured the starvation of Ravensbrück, my grandfather would often find the choicest morsel of food on his plate and place it on hers saying, 'This is for you Dulinka, please eat it,' and she would say, 'No darling, you eat it,' and I would watch bemused as this tender piece of meat would make its way from plate to plate while everyone laughed that it would be stone cold by the time it was decided who would eat it. I remember venturing down to the cellar to find it packed from floor to ceiling with emergency tinned food, a practice common amongst those Poles who had suffered such deprivation.

Chapter 2

At age four I was taken to St Polycarp's Primary School in Bear Lane, Farnham. I remember being told by my grandfather on my first day to behave myself or I would be locked up in a dungeon. I cried uncontrollably at being left there, even though he assured me that I would be picked up by my mother at the end of the school day. Knowing how silly she was I was convinced she would forget and I would never see any of my family again.

I didn't speak a word of English, except for learning one useful phrase my grandfather taught me: 'I beg your pardon.' He told me to use it all the time, but it proved of scant worth to me in the playground. They didn't even teach me to ask where the lavatory was and at times I needed it very much indeed so I cried some more. I had been brought up completely unused to the company of other children and so I didn't want to play 'chase' which I thought was daft. The teacher made me sit in the front row in class and whenever she turned her back to write something on the blackboard I would make a dash for the door and try to escape, only to be hauled back.

At the end of the day my mother was waiting at the school gates and I beamed with such happiness to see her but was horrified to hear that I had to return there the next day. Every day someone would take me to school and I always begged and begged them not to forget to collect me later and even my father was amused and would tell the guests at Sunday teatime. It was a great joke to them but I didn't think it was funny.

One morning, maybe a fortnight later, my grandfather took me to school and I was so demented with anxiety that he obviously had pangs of nerves at leaving me. Unbeknown to me, he went around the side of the building and found a ladder which he climbed having worked out which was my classroom. Wanting to check on me he peered through the window, which was set up high near the ceiling. I had calmed down a bit and remember sitting there forlornly hiccupping with sorrow when I suddenly looked up and saw his face. I let out a roar of anguish and he disappeared having quickly scrambled down. The teacher rushed out and a great commotion followed. I expect he said 'I beg your pardon'.

Some days later I was seated sobbing as usual and obviously the teacher couldn't cope so she asked the headmistress for help. A fearsome figure of authority led me by the hand to her office and sat me on the floor next to a heater and gave me a book with lovely pictures while she sat quietly working at her desk. I instinctively knew I was on to a good thing and did not make a sound. The next day she did the same and I felt very important but then she must have decided to return me to my class.

In December I turned five years old and by then my English was fluent and I was happily settled into the routine. Young brains are like sponges and I learnt fast. By the time I had been at the school for a few weeks I realised that English people didn't like Polish people very much. One day nearing winter all the little girls were told to go to the lavatories which were cubicles at the end of the playground. As it was so cold we were told not to take our coats off and in the small space I had trouble undressing and using the thin, scratchy lavatory paper and I am ashamed to say I made a mess on my coat. I am not sure how it happened but I do remember a teacher cleaning me up afterwards and constantly muttering 'dirty, little foreigner' while I looked at her with solemn, sullen hatred and confusion.

Whilst during my formative years I was subjected to a torrent of abuse at school for being Polish, nevertheless my grandparents and father, despite being unfailingly polite and courteous to all English people at all times, were just as racist towards the English. They would never under any circumstances whatsoever permit me to play with English children or visit their houses. I was not allowed any English friends and they used to provide me with 'suitable' Polish children from good families. It was not even debatable, it was a rule. I grew up very confused encountering all this racial prejudice. I was exasperated by this but, being obedient, I had to do as I was told, especially when very young.

The journey from St Polycarp's to Lawday Place was about ten minutes by bus straight up Castle Street. They must have come to some agreement at the school that a teacher would walk me safely to the bus stop, hand me over to the driver and within minutes we would be at a bus stop outside the gates of the house where my father or someone would be waiting so I didn't have to cross the road by myself. This worked very well for a time but one day the following summer I remember being left in the queue. It was such a wonderfully sunny day that I decided to walk and toddled off. I think somebody half-heartedly tried to stop me but I waved them away and walked and walked. Farnham is a beautiful, old town and I remember seeing a lady in the garden of one of the Georgian houses tending her flowers and I stopped briefly to say how nice they were. Thereafter it was a disaster. I passed by the medieval Farnham castle on the right and kept walking but had totally misjudged the timing and the distance. It only took a few minutes by bus but not so on short, little five-year-old legs and here I was walking in blistering heat along a deserted country road with no pavement, just open countryside. I became very tired, hot and thirsty and a bit frightened, especially when I could hear police sirens coming my way so I hid low down in the long grassy ditch which ran alongside the road not realising that these were my rescuers. My poor father had met the bus and finding me not on it was frantic with worry and a big search operation was mounted.

Eventually, hours later, I reached Lawday Place and remember staggering up the cool, shady drive barely conscious with exhaustion and seeing my grandfather halfway down near the gateway, his face gaunt with worry and then relief. He scooped me up in his arms and carried me to the house, gave me some water and put me straight to bed and told me to pretend to be asleep. Sometime later the door opened and he and my father came into the room and I heard my grandfather saying with reassuring normality, 'don't spank her, poor little thing. Here she is, all safe and sound fast asleep.' Then they went out, my father first and my grandfather following. He turned around and I kept my eyes shut until the last minute, at which point we looked at each other and he winked at me. This episode was told and retold by him to just about everyone for the rest of his life. I thought my grandfather was wonderful, especially as once when I got attacked by a fierce, enormous turkey which landed on my head, he grabbed it and saved me.

I don't remember where my mother was that day. My parents were well and truly divorced by then, but I wasn't bothered as I was part of a huge household of kind adults, so I had no reason to feel uncertain or confused. I think my mother didn't enjoy living in the countryside with her parents-in-law and preferred the bright lights of London.

She had met a distinguished friend of my grandfather's called Mr Henryk who worked at the Foreign Office. He was a childless widower, around fifty years old, and he said he first set eyes on me one sunny Sunday when he came to Lawday Place for lunch; my mother called me from the garden, so I came thrashing out of some bushes covered in mud with twigs in my hair and a runny nose with snot dripping down on to my lip. I was very embarrassed when he used to repeat this story in future years.

I also at this time had a pet magpie which followed me everywhere squawking and terrifying my grandparents' guests, especially some pathetic couple who had a baby in a pram and were frightened my pet bird might do it some harm. My grandmother didn't like it much either as it often flew into the kitchen when I was there and its wing span was quite alarming. Mr Henryk always said I made an unforgettable impression on his mind as when we met I was all filthy with a wild bird on my shoulder.

I think he wanted to civilise me and, after the incident of my solitary walk from Farnham, he advised my mother that I would be safer surrounded and supervised by Catholic nuns. So I was suddenly uprooted aged six from my idyllic surroundings and sent to La Sagesse convent in north London. My much-loved magpie was taken by train in a cardboard box to London and let go in Hyde Park and I cried bitterly. My mother told me that it made friends with other birds in the park straight away, but I didn't believe her.

Despite being very exclusive, La Sagesse had cold stone corridors, iron bedsteads in spartan dormitories and fearsome nuns, one of whom 'boxed my ears' on my very first night for talking after lights out. It was my first experience of violence at the age of six. I was to become a weekly boarder and I couldn't understand why I was imprisoned in this bleak institution which had a high wall all around it with broken glass on top. I was rebuked at every turn and punished severely at every opportunity, especially by Sister Agnes; she with the sharp fists coming to clout me regularly for running up the corridor, and other sins. Everything in the Catholic Church is a sin and we were constantly reminded that Jesus died for us suffering on the Cross and that we must suffer also to show how much we love Him. To discipline those girls who dared to argue amongst themselves, the nuns would grab them by the hair and smash their heads together with all their strength. Needless to say, these quarrels were few and far between.

It was forbidden to get out of bed after lights out and if we needed to go to the lavatory we were punished for being naughty. One night I was so desperate for a pee that, not wanting to risk being caught leaving the dormitory, I leant over the side of the bed and picked up my slipper and peed into that instead, replacing it back on the floor.

I no longer felt cherished or indulged; instead I was reminded each day that as a Polish girl I was very lucky to be in a school like this and should be grateful for my food as, because of my family the world had gone to war and England had been bombed.

Incidentally the food was disgusting with stringy, gristly meat with pipes running through it, tasteless boiled potatoes and endless white bread and margarine with jam. I particularly hated the puddings; the great, wobbly pink blancmanges made me gag and the sickly rice pudding and tapioca were torture. I frequently got my ears boxed for not eating and was forced to sit at the refectory table for hours and finish my food, though I refused. I was abandoned to a life of misery pining for my family and soon learnt the uselessness of tears.

None of my little school friends were healthy on this diet and we all seemed to be permanently coughing, covered in boils in varying degrees of eruption and we all had cracks at the corners of our mouths. For the boils the sister matron would apply hot poultices and then wrap the area with a rubber bandage. We frequently had sties on our eyes and the occasional carbuncle. For these Sister Mary Agnes would make us lean over a bowl of boiling water with a towel over our head to trap the steam and she would give us a wooden spoon covered in gauze which we had to dip into the water and hold as close as we could to our pussy carbuncle to 'bring it out'. This was done repeatedly for about an hour with the water being topped up regularly from her kettle. We all had tummy aches or toothaches and earaches but the nuns showed little sympathy and reminded us of the sufferings of Christ.

My father would pick me up 5 p.m. on Friday nights to take me home for the weekend. I would sit waiting for him on a bench by the front door and when the doorbell rang and the nun in charge of door duty on that day would let him in, he would remove his hat, bow low and kiss her hand in greeting. Word must have gone around about his Polish gentleman and gradually more and more nuns would hover around the front door and line up to be thus greeted. These freaky women who ostensibly chose a life of piety and chastity, devoting their entire being to the love of Jesus Christ, nevertheless bewilderingly turned into giggling idiots whenever there was a handsome man around. The following week they would just revert back to sadism.

They were utterly indifferent to our feelings of homesickness. I think I was quite tough and adapted quickly but for overly sensitive, delicate children these experiences would have scarred them for life. And indeed, in 2015 the *Daily Mail* did an article about the damage of sending very young children to boarding school and a few women in their fifties and sixties gave accounts of their mental damage. I read the article with great interest, especially as two women recounted their stories of La Sagesse convent and how the experience had resulted in permanent trauma. I was quite astonished and thought with some satisfaction that I had 'been there, done that, and survived to tell the tale'.

However, at weekends I would go and stay at Mr Henryk's large flat in Wetherby Mansions, Earls Court Square, which had four bedrooms. I was given a good, warm room beyond the kitchen and Mr Henryk showed great interest in my education. My mother lived there too and also a friend of hers called Misia, a poor, young widow with a baby which was fostered out to some people in the country while she worked as a waitress in the Polish Club in Exhibition Road. Mr Henryk was a wealthy man and always a present help in times of trouble. He had a beautiful sitting room, the walls covered in olive-green silk damask, and he would give endless parties there for carefully selected influential friends, political grandees, the Polish aristocracy in exile and all sorts of interesting people who flocked to him as he was an imposing man of dominant personality and charm. My father was always welcome to call and see me and my grandfather would also come regularly on Friday nights when I was home from school. Mr Henryk was of medium height with brown hair and a face reminiscent of Sid James with a sense of humour to match but nothing saucy. He was very dignified and a great snob in the most amusing way. He told me that snobbery is but a pursuit of excellence and if we look down on snobs then that in itself makes us snobs too and that is quite right. The most important thing in life is to have beautiful manners and the finest compliment anyone could receive is to be told they possess beautiful composure and bearing; no boisterousness or bad language as that is very common. Having a formal Polish rearing, albeit in England, I was instructed up until the age of twelve to do a little curtsy when first introduced to an older person and furthermore to kiss the hand of much older women to show respect, though I thought this was taking things a bit far and tried to avoid aged aunts with whiskers and their friends.

Having as a child observed my superiors' general behaviour, I noticed how their friendships politely and cautiously started; and improved, advanced and developed over time. They would progress from calling newcomers Mr and Mrs (surname) to Mr and Mrs (Christian name) and eventually, when they decided to make official their affection, one or the other would be overcome by friendliness and suggest drinking *Brüderschaft* (brotherhood). This was a momentous rite of passage when two people would hold a glass of champagne or vodka, entwine arms and drink simultaneously. It would normally happen at parties when they had been drinking already and so were extra merry. Immediately after they would kiss each other heartily on both cheeks and from that day forward they would be on Christian-name terms. It would always be a very exciting ritual and whoever might be around witnessing the little ceremony would laugh and applaud and cheer loudly.

There was none of this modern over-familiarity which is the curse of the present age, when boundaries are completely blurred and mere acquaintances, and even complete strangers, lurch into using one's Christian name without leave to do so. It is the grossest impertinence to abandon all respect and assume intimacy with the unwilling. Mr Henryk said it showed insincerity and devalued true friendship. To defer to one's superior is as much to proclaim one's impeccable upbringing as it is to recognise theirs and he should know as he was a diplomat. Polish people are ridiculously polite and rarely swear. If they're very annoyed and feel the need to vent their pent-up anger they say *psia kość*, which means 'dog's bone', or *psia krew*, which means 'dog's blood', or if they are really horrified about something they say *o rany boskie*, which means 'oh wounds of Christ'. The worst swear word is *cholera*, which as I child I was never allowed to use. Amusingly, if they're irritated with a person they will say *niech cię kaczka kopnie* which means 'I hope you get kicked by a duck'. Funny people, the Poles, but I was very gently reared; no one ever shouted at me or hit me, it was an affectionate and formal upbringing.

Mr Henryk's home was always full of laughter and on some quiet evenings he would have friends over to play bridge, but I kept out of the way as it was boring. Before a game he often promised to give me half his winnings and indeed, he bought me a small metal safe with a lock and key so I could keep my pocket money in it. He enriched my understanding and appreciation of the world and was a strong influence on my formative years, assuming the role of a father figure. He took me to the Natural History Museum and also regularly to the Odeon cinema in High Street Kensington. I liked epic films like *Ben-Hur* and *Cleopatra*. One Saturday he took me to Harrods and bought me a birdcage with six canaries and made a special bracket on his kitchen wall to display it. He was obviously madly in love with my mother and a ready-made family appealed to him. In his company my mother blossomed with confidence and gaiety.

I had no idea what sex was or indeed which room my mother slept in but I realise now that they were lovers. On one occasion I was allowed to bring my friend Susan home for the weekend and whilst we were larking around in the middle of the night we must have made too much noise and dropped something as next I knew my mother burst into my room quite naked except for a very sheer pink baby-doll negligee which left nothing to the imagination. I was dreadfully embarrassed.

When I was eight I caught chickenpox and was off school for three weeks. Mr Henryk bought me the entire set of Arthur Mee's *Children's Encyclopaedia* and no illness had ever been so pleasant. His kindness to me made the horrors of boarding school somehow bearable.

I did tell him that I was unhappy at the convent but on this occasion he did not understand or say anything sensible except that 'Schooldays will be the happiest days of your life'. The poor man did not understand how these unnatural malicious women mistreated us as they were so demure and godly when meeting adults. To this day I retain a dislike of the Catholic Church and consider it an abomination that these malevolent women should impose a regimented life of prayer, penance and punishment on very young girls.

During long holidays my father would collect me from school and take me to Waterloo Station where we would meet my grandfather under the clock and I was transported with joy to go to my beloved Lawday Place again. My father, having an impressive command of many European languages, had recently got a job as manager of the export bureau at Harrods. I don't expect it was very well paid but it was prestigious and he was always beautifully dressed for the role. I know he was frequently called upon as an interpreter and being a handsome fellow he was a great success with Harrods' female staff.

My grandfather told me that Mr Henryk had come to see him especially to plead the case for persuading my mother to marry him; otherwise 'whatever will Basia grow into'. But my mother was flighty and frivolous and in no hurry to enter into any marriage. She had freedom, beautiful clothes and pearls and I hardly ever saw her, though occasionally she would come and kiss me goodnight before going to a party rustling in taffeta and smelling of Jean Patou Joy perfume. One time Mr Henryk gave me a test. He asked me which of my parents did I prefer and if my father was at one end of the room and my mother at the other and both were calling me, then which one would I choose to go to. I pondered this for a bit and then with a flash of inspiration I said I would stand in the middle of the room and not move. I felt so proud of my tact that when I next saw my mother, the both of us sitting in the kitchen, I proudly told her this tale. To my horror she burst into hysterical tears and accused me of not loving her. I had never seen her cry before and as she sobbed with her head in her hands upon the kitchen table, I wordlessly went up and put my hand on her shoulder but she waved me away and told me how ungrateful I was. I was speechless with shock that I had upset her so thoughtlessly and don't remember what happened to the rest of the day as I was so mortified. My mother always reacted bafflingly badly whenever my father's name was bought up. She demanded that I dislike him and considered it a great betrayal of her if I ever said I wanted to see him, which I thought was bewildering as I loved him too. Whenever the subject of my father was broached, she would repeat the gesture with her little finger saying, 'he's only got one this big.'

Being an only child, with no brothers, I had never seen a naked boy or man, so had no idea what their private parts looked like. At school, however, when we were at art appreciation classes, I looked at the tiny willies in religious paintings of baby Jesus and little St John the Baptist.

Chapter 3

My mother, though silly, was smart, resourceful and pleasantly crafty with buckets of charm. She somehow managed to convince the owner of a chemist in Cromwell Road that she had qualified in pharmacy at a university though she had in fact only finished high school. I remember when she went for her job interview up to the first floor and told me to sit alone on the stairs by the street and eat my Mars bar and wait. Then I remember her returning, smiling broadly, with the owner following her, also grinning. He patted me on the head and asked if I was a good girl and gave me a five-pound note. Then he kissed my mother's hand lingeringly, bade her farewell and I could see he was smitten.

There was an old woman called Mrs Zosia already working as a qualified pharmacist and she must have tutored my mother swiftly to read doctor's prescriptions and dispense appropriate remedies. I was so proud of my mother in her pristine white starched coat as she efficiently went about healing the sick. I would often dart behind the counter and sit on the stool in the pharmacy section at the back and was fascinated by the selection of little round pillboxes and neat bottles. Occasionally I would sit at the front of the chemist while many persons used to describe their ailments and ask her opinion and she would recommend lotions and potions and nod her head with sympathy. It was the only Polish chemist in London and I suspect many gentleman customers just came to flirt.

Amongst the Polish community it was rumoured that Dr Klupt had bought his doctorate on the black market and therefore knew nothing. But he exuded such kindly Jewish humanity, being a large man and cosy with his snow-white hair, that little old ladies would

Mother Anguish

beg for a consultation with him too and good naturedly he would emerge from his office and sooth the most anxious patient. All in all, his chemist was a hub of Polish activity and he and my mother bluffed their way into everyone's hearts. I think the only person who knew what they were doing was the wise old woman, Mrs Zosia, and I can only surmise that she prevented anyone getting poisoned accidentally. Dr Klupt was a friend of Mr Henryk's and a group was often arranged to lunch together at the Polish Club in Exhibition Road. I always enjoyed being included, especially as Dr Klupt would give me another five-pound note and Mr Henryk would talk me through the intricacies of a French menu and teach me about wine, though I wasn't allowed to drink any as I was only eight. He bought me Schloer apple juice and I rewarded him with love and gratitude and a great eagerness to learn. I valued his opinion on all matters.

The men flocked around my beautiful mother; at the chemist, in restaurants and in the street, frequently a gentleman acquaintance would come up and greet her. Having removed his hat he would stand clutching it to his chest while they exchanged pleasantries and then part, with him kissing her hand as she fluttered her eyelashes and tilted her head. I would watch, enchanted by her grace and feminine assurance and, realising the certainty of female power, I longed to grow up and have a string of admirers myself. She attracted much attention at Mr Henryk's soirees from his distinguished acquaintances and at some time she began an affair with a Mr Ambrose Nevill-Parker who used to buy her orchids and often give me a fiver as well. As a child I thought him incredibly posh and I couldn't imagine her marrying an Englishman but I often wished she would so that I would be able to pass myself off as an English child. Having been born and brought up in England I didn't feel in the slightest bit Polish, although I loved my grandparents and family very much. They spoke funny English and I was sometimes embarrassed when I heard them speaking to

English people, having experienced much racism already. I wanted to be an ordinary English girl, preferably called Lucy. I wasn't then remotely interested in my father having a title in his native land and being an heir to great wealth. It was all in the past and I wanted to fit in and belong to the country in which I was born. It was only much later in my life, upon visiting the medieval splendour of Krakow and viewing my family's vast estate for myself, that I fully embraced my Polish heritage.

My mother also formed a great emotional attachment to a Mr Kieconski who had been an air force pilot in the Battle of Britain. Tall, urbane, imposing, with an exquisitely magnetic personality, he was of Polish-Swedish ancestry and in his mid-fifties. My mother, who would have been around twenty-seven, never went for young men. Mr Kieconski had an antique-furniture shop in Glendower Place, SW7 where he would work in the basement applying mouldings and decorations to what had previously been hideously ugly items bought cheap at auctions. He would then paint them pale cream, add some gold leaf and bingo, he'd created items of great beauty. Sometimes he let me play in his workshop amongst the wood shavings and delicious smells of linseed oil and plaster. And in the late afternoon he would take me to Daquise coffee bar in Thurloe Street for tea and Polish doughnuts.

When Mr Henryk wasn't driving me back to school on Sunday nights, Mr Kieconski drove me and my mother. I remember it was usually dark and I was always sad to be leaving them as I sat in the back of the car with my arms around my mother's neck kissing the back of her head. She had lustrous dark hair and as a special treat she would allow me to spend the whole journey brushing it. I adored Mr Kieconski almost as much as I adored Mr Henryk. They were both gentlemanly, unfailingly amusing with the latest jokes and, being childless widowers, I knew each was as desperate to marry my mother as the other. She strung them along with gaiety and charm and we all seemed like one big, happy family, with me at the epicentre to be spoilt and adored. One summer we all went to Italy for a week together.

Mr Kieconski lived in Lupus Street, Pimlico, SW1 and I detected a strong degree of familiarity between him and my mother, as she behaved totally as if in her own home there and would act as official hostess at his parties. Around this time she told me he had a very large penis but I did not know what that was and I didn't ask; I just looked at her blankly. Other times, she would mention one gentleman as having a bigger one than another gentleman, but I thought she was talking about their cars.

My mother never really worried about me running wild in the streets alone as I was very independent and she had allowed it since I was about six years old. The only condition was that if I wanted to cross the road I had to ask an adult to see me across safely. As we lived within walking distance of the Natural History Museum, I used to go there nearly every day in holiday time and happily wander about looking at all the exhibits, especially the dinosaurs, although I was very sad to see a stuffed baby elephant. At eight years old I was streetwise enough to scuttle from where I lived in refined South Kensington to North End Road Market and there I found a pet shop with black Labrador cross puppies gambolling in a window. They cost £2 each and I begged my mother for one but she said no.

When I was ten, my father decided to buy me an elegant Pekingese puppy. I was unsure about the breed, as I had only associated them with little old ladies and wanted a black Labrador instead, but we caught the Tube to Highgate one evening to see an elderly lady called Miss Springett. She ushered us into her sitting room and said, 'Wait here and I shall get the baby.' She spread a newspaper over her carpet, left the room and returned with a squiggling brown furry ball, six-inches wide and six-inches long, which she placed on the floor. I fell in love with it immediately. My dad paid £10 and we came home with 'Trusie' tucked into his inner jacket pocket. She grew into a loving creature; Pekingese are supremely clever dogs, they have an extra bit to their brain.

Around this time my parents divorced due to my father's affair with a woman called Kitty Lubicz, who I never met. Apparently Mr Lubicz found out and they both went to live in Canada. My mother and I had set up a permanent home with Mr Henryk but her and my father remained ostensibly on good terms as my father was determined not to lose touch with me whether my mother liked it or not. We lived in Wetherby Mansions for three years and My Henryk liked my doggy as well. Trusie would recognise the sound of my dad's car from way down the road whenever he came to visit and grew hysterical with excitement before he had even parked. We took her for lovely walks in Kensington Gardens and she would leap on to sleeping tramps and courting couples. When I was at school Mr Henryk would look after Trusie.

When I was eleven, we moved out of Wetherby Mansions. My mother got a mortgage and bought a two-bedroom, one-sitting room and one-dining room flat in Bramham Gardens close by, on the other side of Earls Court Road. It was a first-floor flat, split-level, with a balcony at the front and a fair sized terrace overlooking the communal gardens at the back. We moved in and I was very excited that my mummy and I had a place of our very own. I so much wanted to involve myself with the upkeep that one day when she was out I went to the hardware shop and bought a mop and some Flash floor cleaner with my pocket money. I must have scrubbed too hard at the new linoleum on her beautiful kitchen floor as the top layer of pale blue colour came right off, exposing brown cork underneath. It was completely destroyed and she must have been dismayed as it had only just been laid the day before but she wasn't angry with me. In those times she was always very good natured. Whenever I was home in the evenings, Mr Kieconski would always come for dinner, which mother cooked deliciously. He had his own keys to our flat, so my memories are of him just entering the kitchen with a smile, always with a bottle of wine in his pocket.

The following summer Mother, Mr Henryk, Mr Kieconski and some others all went to Spain together while I was sent to spend the holiday with my grandparents at Lawday Place, which was fine by me. I don't know whether my mother indulged in any degree of upper-class debauchery with these men as I was far too busy being a child. I remember that, to my consternation, she developed a serious crush on a man called Conrad. I found him passably agreeable, handsome but a bit creepy. He gave me a kitten as a present but it didn't get on with Trusie so we had to give it back. My mother behaved all silly when Conrad was around but she told me she wasn't going to marry him as he had once said that it didn't matter if she grew old eventually as by then 'Basia will be grown up and ready for him'. I didn't quite know why she was so furious, although she frequently brought up in conversation that women age far quicker than men. Her looks were all she had to lift her up in life and she had to capitalise on them while they lasted. She often mentioned that she was worried about the 'change of life' which would happen eventually but I didn't know what that was either.

Then, one Christmas when I was twelve, Mr Henryk, who loved to cook, invited us for Christmas Eve late lunch at about 4 p.m. Mr Kieconski, Mum and I arrived all jolly and in high spirits bearing wine and a scarf I had knitted him in his favourite maroon colour. His flat was on the third floor and we went up in the lift and could smell the roast dinner as soon as we got to his door. We rang the doorbell but no answer came. We rattled the letter box, called through it cheerfully that we were there and for a joke we all sang 'Jingle Bells' as loud as we could. After a while we presumed that he must have run out of mustard or some ingredient and gone to the shops on Brompton Road, so we happily waited. At last we heard the lift coming and said 'let's give him a fright', so when the doors opened we leapt up and all shouted 'boo'. Two policemen got out and said they had come to see the next of kin of Mr Henryk, to which we explained that we were here for Christmas dinner. 'I am very sorry to tell you,' one of the policemen said, 'but Mr Henryk has just had a heart attack and died in the street.' My mother gasped and I turned to the wall in shock and banged my head against it a few times, crying and exclaiming, 'oh no, oh no!' It was my first experience of death and of losing someone so beloved by me. A titan of my existence, gone in a flash. Gone forever. I still keep a photograph of him on my bookcase to this day. Whenever I am in that neighbourhood, I always think of him and wonder what on earth made him leave the house when he knew we were coming. Why did he have to go down the road and whereabouts in that street did he clutch his chest and fall? I always wonder who was there and who might have helped him and it's heart breaking to think that he was rushing to see me and my mother at the time. He would have been so anxious and we were not with him to hold his hand as he died.

I have no knowledge of the dinner getting burnt or what happened to it but we left utterly stricken and staggered into a nearby hotel inconsolably upset. I was given a gin and tonic, my first alcoholic drink. Christmas must have come and gone; my mother wept, I went to Granny's and never attended his funeral. I wasn't told when it was and I was too shell-shocked to ask, but I would have liked to have gone. I was just sent away and we never spoke of him again; it would have been too painful to reminisce and besides, I didn't have the words. My mother never mentioned anything apart from that he had left her everything in his will. I still own his glass-fronted bookcase and a little wooden piggy-shaped corkscrew, the pig's tail being the screw. To this day I think of him whenever I use it.

School resumed and life went on. My mother and Mr Kieconski drove me back at the beginning of term with my trunk, tuck box and other paraphernalia. That day my mother had a dreadful black eye as two nights before I was demonstrating the rules of hockey to her in our sitting room and swung my stick right into her face. But she wasn't cross and enjoyed telling people how I had biffed her and smashed her on the head. Halfway through the term she wrote to me that Mr Kieconski had gone away somewhere on holiday but did not know where. I was a bit unsettled and thought this was odd as they were inseparable and always holidayed together. I was a full boarder now but still allowed out for tea two Sundays in a term. The following Sunday she came to take me out for tea, this time being driven by another admirer called Oswald, but the atmosphere was tense. I missed Mr Kieconski very much and at one point, sitting in the back of the car, I asked if she knew where he had gone. She remained silent, exchanging glances with Oswald. I felt a dreadful chill but spoke no more. Instinctively I knew something was wrong.

Three weeks later it was the holidays, so I came home to Bramham Gardens and on the first day my mother patted the sofa and said, 'come and sit down by me, I have to tell you something.' I immediately turned sharply and said, 'who has died?' 'Mr Kieconski,' she replied. 'I knew it, I knew it,' I cried and sat down and we both sobbed. He had died of a heart attack, alone in his flat in Lupus Street. My mother had not heard from him and he had not come for dinner the night before, so she went to check his flat and found him dead on the floor by the side of his bed. I did not go to his funeral because it had already taken place three weeks earlier in June when I was at boarding school. Mother didn't want me to be upset before my exams so I was told nothing. She said his grave was a long way away, not in our local Brompton Cemetery, so I never got to see it. Something makes me think he was cremated and she didn't want to tell me.

I was horrified that our two greatest protectors were both gone within six months of each other. Who would care for us now I thought? Who would make us laugh, who would come around for dinner and crack jokes and help me with my Latin? I felt crippled with anxiety about our future. It was hard enough having to work so many things out for myself without a sensible mother. She never even saw herself in that role, always wanting to be my friend instead. Mother bought us a two-week package tour to Riccione, Italy but there was no joy in travelling; we just went by ourselves and I looked after her as she looked after me while we muddled along in a three-star *pensione*, which was all we could get at the last minute. We spoke to no one at the beach and at the hotel dinner table we ate our meals in silence. One evening, some man had delivered a large bunch of red roses for her and we found them on our table. She obviously had an admirer. Men stared at her in the street and when one went so far as to pinch her bottom I was livid with outrage and spat at him.

There was no immediate cause for financial worry due to Mr Henryk's will. She returned to working at the chemists, no longer her ebullient self. Our flat was our haven but there were reminders of Mr Henryk and Mr Kieconski everywhere, especially the latter as we had furnished it completely with his style of white, cream and gold. My mother's friend Misia came to live with us too. We never ever spoke of either of the men and I spent my holidays wandering the streets of London in a daze of grief. I regularly went to the Wetherby Mansions front door as a pilgrimage and just looked through the letter box. Mr Henryk was buried in Brompton Cemetery just around the corner and I would plant flowers around his grave. I still visit it to this day.

The months passed and I changed boarding school. As in my first experience we were not fed properly by the nuns and also I developed terrible chilblains on my toes. They itched and hurt awfully for weeks but I just accepted the pain as I did not know what it was. On Sunday afternoons all the girls had to go for a long, healthy walk in the country air and my toes were excruciatingly sore. Upon returning to the school building, having limped for hours, I thought I would take my sock off to check out the pain. All my toes were purple like swollen plums but the one on my little toe had burst and a chunk of my flesh came away stuck to the sock as I pulled it off. I showed Matron who applied ointment and bandaged me up and the next day called for the doctor who gave me antibiotics as my little toe bone was exposed. When I went home for the holidays I remember sitting on the bed with my foot in my mother's lap as she smeared on more ointment and cried at the sorry state my feet were in. To this day I don't understand why she didn't make a formal complaint. She was a bit pathetic and nervous when dealing with persons of authority, but even so the school had been hideously expensive and for that money you don't expect your kid's toes to nearly drop off. Getting around was very inconvenient for me as my feet had been so heavily bandaged that I couldn't get my shoes on.

As if I didn't have enough problems I was suffering a crisis of confidence as the result of my appearance. While I was a cute little child, my development towards adolescence had not been so pretty and I was devastated when one of my breasts began to develop and the other stayed completely flat, remaining so until the age of fourteen. This singled me out for terrible bullying from the other girls. Often they would dare each other to rush across to my bed after lights out and squeeze my only breast. They also made me terribly worried by convincing me that my existing boob would grow to twice the size to compensate for the one which wasn't there. This misery was compounded by the glasses I was incorrectly prescribed for short-sightedness, which brought on severe dizziness, as well the ugly pigtails ruthlessly enforced by the nuns, who considered any loose hair to be very 'immodest' and wouldn't even allow a ponytail. Hair had to be neatly plaited and kept away from the face and I once cut a tiny little fringe on one side and got severely punished as fringes were 'immoral'.

Pigtails, glasses and one tit; I was a sorry sight. My mother's approach was hardly reassuring either. She sent me into a terrible panic by suggesting that I might never be able to breastfeed when I grew up and had children. This was very much typical of her as she used to become quite hysterical too at the slightest irregularity in my menstrual cycle and in the end I learned to ignore this unnecessarily dramatic behaviour. She was also very much embarrassed by me during my ugly phase and once when we went together to a Polish shop she made me stand out in the street and wait for her instead of coming in, just in case she met some Polish person she knew; truly a role reversal with her playing the part of the adolescent. I wasn't cross about this, I certainly didn't want to embarrass her and as I was her genetic by-product, I knew I was supposed to look good.

At the new school I felt unsettled and did not flourish. I had always been top of the class and thought exams a wonderful game since, with the exception of maths, I always came first but suddenly I was at the very bottom. It must have been a manifestation of emotional distress. After my initial interview, I was placed into the top stream of form three but did so poorly academically in my depressed state that I was frequently punished and then suffered the ghastly humiliation of being put down a year to the lowest stream of form two with all the halfwits and dunderheads. I was too horror-struck to complain and in retrospect should have worked extra hard to show them I was capable of a return to form three but I was sullen and resentful and avoided everybody. This was especially apparent in my attitude to the headmistress, Sister Mary Agatha, who I know also didn't like Polish people. When calling me out in assembly, she used to mispronounce my name on purpose. She also had an unerring intuition when it came to recognising boys' handwriting on envelopes and would always open such letters with the scissors she had jangling from a chain she wore around her waist. Aged twelve I got a valentine and she took me aside and said to me 'we don't want your type of girl here' and told me that I was never to write to boys or have boys write to me. I was gutted at this injustice as I had no idea who the valentine had come from. I also objected to the insulting label 'that type of girl', though without much clue as to what it might suggest.

At the chemist, one of the regular customers was a sinister-looking man called Stefan who used to pick up medication for his terminally ill wife Jadwiga. He had obviously noticed my mother for a while, although she had no recollection of him. As soon as he found out that her lover Mr Kieconski had died he took his chance and asked if he might call and visit her. Bramham Gardens is an odd street; the other side of the road is called Bolton Gardens where Stefan owned a large six-storey house directly opposite us without our realising. On the appointed day, my mother and I stood at the window in silence, watching him emerge out of his dark green Jaguar and at this point she realised he was indeed very wealthy. She needed to make an advantageous marriage as she was now thirty-one years old and not getting any younger, as she kept telling me. It was inconceivable to me that this glum, ugly, predatory neighbour could be a suitable candidate. He rang the doorbell and came up to the first floor. He was of medium height and had strange slanted eyes and slicked-back brown hair. He brought a box of chocolates, tied in a purple bow, and we sat making awkward, stilted conversation, punctuated by uncomfortable silences. He told us that the house opposite was inhabited by tenants and a housekeeper called Mrs Lovelace who lived in the basement with her husband and two little sons. The wiring was antiquated, he said, and one of the little boys had wet himself in the night, soaking his pyjamas, so when he switched on the light he electrocuted himself and ended up in hospital. It was a beautiful house on the outside and would be worth a fortune today, I've been told.

Stefan's wife had just died and he lived in a two-and-a-half-floor maisonette in Elvaston Place just off Queen's Gate. Stefan invited us to lunch the following Sunday at the Brompton Grill in Knightsbridge and my mother made silly conversation while I remained silent as no one spoke to me. Polish children are usually very well mannered and never speak unless spoken to first. There was no humour in him at all, he was very unattractive, a taciturn man, ill at ease and I suspect shy.

I told my father about him and he said he had heard of this misfit who was nevertheless undoubtedly the richest Polish man in England, having made his money by buying up many properties in London during the Blitz. Apparently he was held in contempt by the Polish community as he hadn't taken part in the war and had in the meantime made his fortune, though perhaps that wasn't his fault as he was very short sighted, had flat feet, a heart murmur and also a major abdominal hernia. Perhaps we should have all been sorry for him; he wasn't to blame for being knock-kneed and unable to see where he was going. My mother's mother, Anna, who lived in Gloucestershire, also came for the Sunday lunch and she didn't like him either. Later that day she told me he had confided in her to having fallen in love with my mother like a crazy person but even so I hoped my mother would never have lunch with him again.

After another cold, bleak Christmas holiday, I suffered a miserable journey back to boarding school and didn't give him a second thought. I was too depressed to apply myself to my studies and the highlight of each day was when Sister Mary of the Sacred Heart (Smotsh for short) came out with a batch of letters after lunch. We congregated as she read our names out; such joy for news from home and my mother wrote regularly. One day my name was called and I clutched my precious letter and went to my dormitory to read it in private. Inside was a formal printed announcement stating that she had married Stefan on 18 February at Chelsea Registry Office and there was also a short covering letter to me to say that they were now honeymooning in Paris at the Ritz.

Mother Anguish

I was thunderstruck with shock that she had actually got married without telling me and roared like an animal while running down the corridor, as if to get away from the news. A couple of other girls opened their doors to investigate the noise and I remember one prefect coaxing me into her room where I showed her the card and wept hysterically saying that he was an old man and my mother was only thirty-one. Then I stopped myself; I had never admitted to anyone that my parents were divorced, so how could I now explain this shameful new marriage? Lunch break was only one hour, so I went to my classroom speechless and I remember that for no reason whatsoever I fell off my chair during geography and crashed to the ground. I swiftly got up without an explanation. Perhaps someone tittered, I don't remember but from then onwards I carried on as normal and did not mention my news to anyone at all. I don't know if the prefect said anything to the others but I avoided them all as I felt stupid.

Just before the Easter holidays, my mother wrote to inform me that we now lived in Elvaston Place and sent me a map of how to get to our new home. I caught the train to King's Cross and then the Tube to Gloucester Road station, which is two stops away from Earls Court, where we had lived at Bramham Gardens, so not too far. I walked along with my satchel and all my luggage. I arrived and rang the doorbell and I remember my mother being beautifully dressed and coiffed as she let me in. She looked like a multi-millionaire's wife already. Then she led me upstairs as I lugged my trunk. Although thereafter I lived in Stefan's maisonette for six years, I was never allowed to use that main door again. A new door higher up on the communal staircase had been knocked through, so I had my own entrance close to where my bedroom was on the second floor. Downstairs on the first floor, it was a very handsome residence: the sitting room was the most lavishly furnished room I had ever seen, with exquisite antiques and three large arched French windows which opened on to a balcony; then there was a dining room, a conservatory and a corridor leading to the kitchen and the back of the house where Stefan had his own snug bedroom measuring about ten square feet. All the doors on this level were arched and gilded. An indoor spiral staircase led to a mezzanine landing which housed a bathroom, lavatory and a small room converted into an extra kitchen for Misia, who came to live with us also. My mother could not bring herself to abandon her and besides she and Stefan intended to travel a lot so it was sensible to have someone living in the house. From the landing another staircase climbed to the upper floor and my mother's beautiful bedroom. It was spacious and decadent with a king-sized bed, a chaise longue, a large, ornate mantelpiece, pink and beige brocade curtains with golden tassels and an en suite dressing room. Across the corridor was my room. I had never had a large room of my own before and was pleased with it, especially as all of dear Mr Kieconski's furniture taken with us from Bramham Gardens was piled into it, filling it with good but sad memories. My room was very crowded indeed, with two large wardrobes, three chests of drawers, a dressing table and bench, a bookcase, two chairs, a long cabinet on which stood the television and a large desk with a flip lid. And of course my bed was also somehow crammed in against the wall. It was so overcrowded that I kept stubbing my toe for lack of walking room.

My mother instructed me to always let myself in by the upstairs door with my own latch key and never to come downstairs and bother her when Stefan was in the house. I was to keep out of his way at all times and never ever let him see me as he hated me very much. She told me that she would bring my food up to me so there was no need for me to go down to the kitchen. As for my breakfast, I could walk down to a cafe in Gloucester Road. My mother forbade me from using the phone as Stefan would not like it and under no circumstances was I to give our telephone number to any of my friends as Stefan would despise anyone ringing for me. I was also told not to use the lavatory or the bathroom too often as the landing was immediately above the kitchen where Stefan, who didn't want to hear the chain flushing, used to like sitting at the table, drinking black coffee and puffing his cigar. So as much as possible I was to use the cafe down the road and if I needed to make a phone call I was to use the phone box which stood by the corner of Elvaston Place and Gloucester Road. 'A gentleman's home is his castle,' she declared. I asked why Stefan hated me so and she explained that I was the living proof that she had been to bed with another man and he was jealously possessive. Huh. Little did he know, I thought to myself, about all of the others. At least she and my father were lawfully married; it's not as though I was a bastard child.

I felt bewildered and insulted and just a bit like Mrs Rochester kept at the top of the house. I was an intruder in what was supposed to be my own home. However, I adjusted to the new circumstances and it was nice to have a television all to myself. My mother also told me never to see my own father again, as Stefan again would not like it, but I felt that, since I was now twelve, I should do as I liked and my dad only lived nearby in Courtfield Gardens. I rang my dad and we met up. I found out that a few days earlier he had come calling to see me at my new address but when Stefan opened the door to see who it was, he had slammed the door in my father's face. Having been refused entry, my father had left a bag of fruit for me on the floor by my front door. My poor daddy. I felt heartbroken for him that he had been thus treated and he told me he had been aghast that his ex-wife had married such a revolting man for his money. My father told me that a few days before her marriage he had bumped into my mother in the street and when she had told him of her impending nuptials, he begged her not to do it, using the adage, 'how many eggs can you have for breakfast?' My father used to like these old sayings and come up with things like 'two spoons of sugar in your tea is lovely but twenty spoons is disgusting'.

At least my little dog, bought for me by Father for my tenth birthday, was happy. She would sit on the balcony all day long with her head poking through the balustrade watching the world go by. Whenever she saw me approaching on the street, her head would bob joyfully and I often thought she might hurtle from the balcony with excitement. I loved that dog and Stefan seemed to like her too, praising her for matching the oriental furniture in his sitting room. He had a big round pouffe and in the evenings when they had guests, the dog would sit in the middle decoratively. She slept in the kitchen next to Stefan's room. My mother said I was not allowed to take Trusie upstairs to my bedroom, as Stefan would not like it now that he considered her his own but I often encouraged her to run up with me when he was out.

Stefan hated the thought of me visiting my grandfather, my usual holiday routine, as he detested 'heroes'. As the holidays progressed, I quickly realised that he was systematically bullying my mother and controlling every aspect of her life. I observed her becoming meek, submissive, anxious and timid. Sometimes she would come upstairs to my room in the evening to cry and complain bitterly about him, but she always finished on the note that he is an old man, who drinks and smokes too much and soon he will be dead and we will have all his money. I found this sentiment appalling, despite my abhorrence of the man, and was utterly perplexed. Her character had changed entirely from the cheerful, vivacious woman that she was in the days of Mr Henryk and Kieconski, days filled with her laughter. No laughter at all rang out in this house now and she had become subservient and hyperactively eager to please him. I was horrified by this and also noticed to my concern that she was beginning to drink too much. Observing my mother's crazy love life from my early childhood and her overwhelming and savage hatred for both her husbands, I always used to announce that when I got married, I would definitely make sure I married a man that I did not love, as that way I would never get hurt.

However, he liked her to look good and was very generous when buying her elegant coats, mink furs and jewellery. He encouraged her to go to the hairdressers in Gloucester Road nearly every day. When I was home from school I went with her and was fascinated by the intricate and artistic way they would put up her hair. After a while I decided I could do just as good a job by watching and copying their techniques and my mother was happy to let me practise on her.

Stefan also started designing dresses for my mother to wear which he copied from movies. She had always been a talented and expert dressmaker and enjoyed being industrious, so indulged him by sewing his patterns. Some were truly beautiful, especially a white chiffon frock with a sequined waistband, but others were a disaster, including one with bits of fur trim sprouting in unlikely places. Stefan foolishly fancied himself as a couturier. I begged my mother to stop working so hard. She had a sewing machine in the back of the conservatory and spent hours bent over her labours.

Having married a trophy wife, Stefan wanted to show her off, so they went out most nights, mainly to the Polish Club in Exhibition Road. Mother and Stefan also entertained a lot at home but I never attended the parties as I wasn't allowed downstairs. Whenever they had guests, he would ask the ladies to dance but astonishingly he had never taken dancing lessons, so whilst inebriated he would just make up the steps as he went along. He used to sway and twizzle with no sense of rhythm and lift his leg up alarmingly across a woman's side as if he was doing a tango. My mother must have been mortified and it was no wonder nobody accepted a second invitation. Stefan had no social graces whatsoever; he had no humour at all, never smiled or cracked a joke. He seemed always to be in a bad mood. He was so silent that on a couple of occasions I thought he was actually out of the house, so I sneaked into the kitchen to make some toast and a cup of tea only to find him sitting there surly and unresponsive, at which point he would ignore me or give me a dismissive look and turn his head away. I would quickly go upstairs again and I never used the kitchen if he was there, no matter how hungry I was.

I began to have my suspicions that my mother was doing her best to turn us against each other; that while she repeatedly told me of Stefan's hatred for me, she had been telling Stefan much the same story and in this way created a wedge. I dare say that this was down to her fear that he'd develop an interest in me the way Conrad had. Possibly if I had had the opportunity to be charming to Stefan the atmosphere would have been different and, as he had no children, he might have looked upon me as a daughter.

Some years before marrying my mother, Stefan had bought a 200-acre farm in North Devon near Combe Martin with beautiful rolling countryside and a stone eighteenth-century farmhouse. It was very isolated and a bolthole for him; my mother said he had bought it to escape his dying wife, Jadwiga, and retreat there to go on his drunken benders. He employed a manager called John who had an unbelievably strong local accent and he ran the farm in Stefan's absence. Stefan had a few hundred head of sheep and a few fields of strawberries. I only went there once during the lambing season and I immensely enjoyed taking the role of John's right-hand woman and helping out in the dead of night as ewes were delivering their lambs just about all at once. However, I thought Stefan was a bit rough as I watched him deliver twin lambs out of a poor labouring ewe. Some of the lambs were rejected by their mothers and we kept them in the barn and fed them bottled baby milk. They always had diarrhoea but I cuddled them anyway.

One day back in London, I was informed that a Mr and Mrs Winter had come for dinner the night before and were so charmed by Trusie sitting on his ornamental pouffe that my new stepfather had given my dog to the beautiful Mrs Winter as a present. Horror-struck, I rang and asked for my dog back but they refused. I rang my dad for help and he was just as distraught but we could do nothing. My mother, totally dominated by her husband, told me that it was for the best and that Trusie would have a better time anyway; I didn't want to make life harder for my mum, especially as she had enough problems, what with my stepfather fancying Mrs Winter. I cried bitterly but resigned myself to this catastrophe. Like a woman giving up her child for adoption, I was thereafter never allowed to visit her and it really was too painful to speak of. Trusie's little bed was still in the kitchen and I wept as I removed her blankets and her toys; she had been my first dog, the dearest, cleverest little dog and I had loved her dearly. Later my mother said that Trusie, who had slept in the kitchen next to Stefan's room, had sometimes annoyed him as she snored and that this was partly to blame. I developed a deep hatred for Stefan and thought, how can he come into our lives causing so much pain and be responsible for my mother's complete change of character, turning her into a pathetic wreck. We had been quite all right before he came along but I suppose she must have felt vulnerable after Mr Henryk and Mr Kieconski's deaths and married him on the rebound.

Stefan developed an interest in photography and spent a ridiculous amount of time photographing my mother in all manner of poses. Not pornographic but certainly erotic and naked. I questioned my mother's wisdom in allowing this as she complained to me that he had put his favourite shots into an album and would show it to his friends. I thought it was undignified and stupid. I started getting exasperated with her, considering her not unlike an unruly teenager that needed keeping in shape. She became very contrary; sometimes she cried and other times she raved about the injustice of life, bemoaning his refusal to die.

She must have been very lonely as she begged him to allow her to return to work for a couple of days a week in the chemist and interact with people cheerfully. He permitted it and I was very pleased. One dark evening in the winter I decided to meet her halfway home and give her a nice surprise. She was delighted to see me and we walked a short distance up Cromwell Road but suddenly I realised that Stefan had also decided to launch a friendly ambush as we met him just turning on to Gloucester Road. He was furious to see me and my mother nervously took his arm to placate him, the two of them walking faster ahead with me trailing forlornly behind, totally ignored. At Stefan's flat we entered by our separate entrances and I decided to run away from a home where I was so unwelcome as soon as I grew up a bit.

Christmas Eve is very important to Polish people and although on ordinary days I was always brought a tray of dinner in my room, an exception was made at Christmas. We went to the Polish Club with their friends Tomasz and Ursula for the traditional nine-course Polish feast. The atmosphere was exuberant, the Christmas tree gigantic and the decorations and music roused one's spirits of patriotism and good will. I was dressed in pale blue lace, a dress handed down after my mother had worn it a couple of times and she had altered it to fit me. She even let me borrow her pearls. I was happy at dinner but spoiled everything when I saw Stefan chewing on a celery stick. I remarked that celery was healthy and good for the teeth. Stefan's face hardened and my mother kicked me under the table. On returning home, she asked how I could say such a thoughtless and rude thing, considering Stefan wore dentures. 'But I had no idea they were false, it never occurred to me,' I protested. My mother then informed me that Stefan always referred to me as an expensive parasite that needed feeding, not to mention his distaste for paying my private school fees, so I simply had to stop offending him.

Whenever he wanted sex, he would go to my mother's room, which was next to mine and I could hear him grunting. I would wait for him to take his pleasure and finish, then hear him leave and walk down the corridor. I remember peering out my bedroom door and seeing the back of him, departing down the corridor in his dressing gown. It always made me feel sad and at these times I wouldn't bother my mother in her room out of courtesy, to allow her to get over it or whatever she needed. I have no idea how she dealt with the conjugal aspect of the marriage and I never asked her as the prospect was ghastly and didn't conjure up a nice image in my mind.

When I was about thirteen, my mother decided to murder Stefan. One night, when he was sleeping in his cosy room next to the kitchen, she turned on all the gas rings on the range, which would have been a couple of yards from his head, left the door open to his bedroom and then shut the kitchen door to the corridor and went upstairs to bed. I knew nothing about this until the next morning, when I was woken by my mother saying, 'come and help, Stefan is almost dead! I didn't mean to do it, I had too much to drink last night.' I ran downstairs and the overwhelming smell of gas made my eyes water and my nose run. Misia came too and all three of us were spluttering and choking. I opened the kitchen window and we dragged the dead weight of an unconscious, blue-faced Stefan out of his bed. He was so heavy we couldn't lift him but bent over and tripping over our trailing dressing gowns, we pulled him along the floor of the corridor. In the sitting room, I opened the French windows on to the balcony, left him on the floor and called 999 and shortly after an ambulance arrived, sirens blazing, but it drove too far up the street. I had the indignity of running into Queen's Gate in my pyjamas and robe to catch them. The ambulance men carted Stefan away to St Mary Abbot's Hospital while my mother and I got dressed in order to follow him, taking his wash bag and essentials. I'll never forget walking down Cromwell Road when she admitted that, fed up with his manipulative, coercive behaviour and bullying tactics, she had had a few drinks and decided to gas him and pretend he had done it accidentally himself. She was a bag of trembling nerves but I supported her as best I could, horrified by her taking such risks. When we were directed to his ward, we saw two policemen standing outside and my mother froze. They explained that in each case of attempted suicide by gassing they were duty-bound to investigate. My mother was near to collapse so I piped up and told the policemen that Stefan was drunk on a daily basis and often put the kettle on the hob for a cup of tea before forgetting to switch the gas off: 'he does that all the time,' I said, 'he's very absent minded.' The police seemed satisfied and Mum and I came home but I told her she was crazy to put all our lives at risk like this, we could have all been blown up, and she said she would never do it again. At least we had the anticipation of a few days peace and quiet on our own in the house as the doctors informed us that they would keep Stefan in hospital for a few days' observation.

The following day, early in the morning, the doorbell rang and there was Stefan furious on the porch, still in his dressing gown, demanding money for the taxi. He had discharged himself from hospital and hailed a cab in the street still in his pyjamas.

Life resumed. Stefan decided to take my mother to Devon for a few weeks but she couldn't cope with the isolation so pretended she had a dental appointment and came home. He was to follow next week. One evening she told me she was going on a date. She had accepted an invitation to dinner by a gentleman who would be calling for her at 7 p.m. She was very excited and I was excited for her; she seemed her old self again, sitting by her dressing table in front of her large silver-framed mirror, applying her make-up. I had fixed her false eyelashes and arranged her hair and she looked ravishingly pretty. I was leaning against the window looking out on a light summer's evening and so pleased that she would be out having a nice time when all of a sudden, as I glanced down into the street, there was Stefan crossing the road. He had returned unexpectedly, maybe to catch her. 'Stefan is coming,' I said in a daze of disbelief. My mother screeched, 'Oh my God, oh my God,' and ran around the room tearing her clothes off, rummaging her hands through her elaborate hairstyle and smudging her make-up.

Mother Anguish

'Get into your dressing gown quick,' I said, 'and I shall ring your bloke and stop him coming.' Alas, he was already on his way so didn't answer his phone. 'Keep Stefan upstairs,' I said and in a blind dash I ran down to the street, bumped into Stefan coming in and without a word of greeting I gabbled that I was just running to the phone box at the end of the road. He went upstairs and I found out later that he immediately asked my mother to come down and help him unpack the car but she detained him upstairs with all manner of excuses and hugs and kisses. Eventually he got impatient.

Meanwhile, I sat anxiously on the front step with a churning stomach for what seemed like hours. Finally a taxi drew up and a beautifully dressed, middle-aged and portly, dark-haired man emerged with a huge bouquet of red roses. I ran to him with the words 'Stefan is back' and he, quicker than a flash, climbed back into the cab and ordered it to drive away at speed. Within seconds, the front door opened and an exasperated Stefan came out with my ashen-faced mother behind him but I gave her a reassuring smiling nod and she knew the crisis had passed and catastrophe averted. For the next few months I was her heroine and she told all her girlfriends, with me present, how I had saved her life. I begged her not to take such risks with other men again and to stop acting like a juvenile delinquent. If she was so unhappy in her marriage, why couldn't we get another flat like Bramham Gardens and live as we did before? But to this she responded that Stefan was so rich, why should she leave her spectacular home for some other woman to enjoy. Stefan was a great womaniser and she was under no illusions as to whether he would quickly replace her. He had grown in confidence having attracted such a pretty wife and no doubt could get another.

Chapter 4

I had few friends in London as the girls from my boarding school tended to be scattered across England and my best friend lived in Northumberland. So I spent my days walking to Harrods etc and my mother always gave me plenty of money. Sometimes I went to the hairdresser to have my hair done beautifully, although I wasn't going out anywhere special as I didn't know anyone and felt irritated when the shampooist routinely asked. I was lonely so I considered this good practise for when I grew up and became a great lady. I also perfected my call to passing taxis and then entered, instructing the driver 'Harrods please' although we lived within walking distance. I was very lost in life and bored.

Often I went to visit my grandfather Tadeusz who was now living in Acton. I was devastated to learn that whilst I was away at school he had sold Lawday Place, finding it too much hard work. I had always thought that we would keep it in the family for ever. All my joyful childhood memories came flooding back and I grieved for that house as for a person. To make matters worse I learnt that he had sold it to some developer who knocked it down and built dozens of hideous bungalows on the site. But whatever happened to my beautiful, big cedar tree? It was too painful to imagine the vandalism which some hateful builder would have perpetrated, destroying all that I held so dear with no notion of my feelings. I loved that tree. And I so loved Lawday Place; before going to sleep at night I would frequently imagine myself going back in time and wandering through the house. I still do, all these years later, and I daydream sentimentally sometimes of building a house of exactly the same design and identical in every way, three staircases and all.

Mother Anguish

I recently Googled Lawday Place and it is now a huge dormitory suburb. All the people who live in all the run of the mill little houses there have no idea whatsoever of the original gracious house that once occupied the grounds and the lovely family that lived there, including a wild little girl who had a pet magpie.

My father was working in Germany most of the time, something to do with the import and export of wine, but otherwise he lived in Courtfield Gardens, SW7 and whenever he was in London my mother flew into a rage and reminded me of how he had an affair with Kitty Lubicz, along with a host of others. She maintained she couldn't understand his success with women as he had such a small willy and as always she would accompany this statement by holding up her little finger while her face took on an ugly twist. Once when I defied her and arranged to meet him for coffee she nagged and nagged me as I was getting ready, reminding me of how many sacrifices she had made to bring me up, how expensive my private schooling was, how disloyal I was to her and claiming that she 'nearly died' giving birth to me and hadn't been able to have a child since as she was so 'ripped about' inside following such a difficult labour. She went on and on about how much it hurt giving birth to me and how I was so ungrateful and didn't love her as much as I should. By the time I met my father, who would have been looking forward to seeing me, she had worked on me so efficiently that she almost had me convinced that he was the most evil of men who had done her untold harm and didn't like me much either or else he wouldn't have run off with blinking Kitty Lubicz. To my eternal shame, I was grumpy with my dad, picked on him during our meal and over nothing I got up and stormed out, leaving him bewildered sitting at the table. In the street I immediately felt that I had done something unpardonably wrong and hurt his feelings but I also felt I had championed my mother, so should be proud. I walked home very depressed and confused and hormonally disturbed as only teenage girls can be. I began to realise that although I loved my mother, she had a venomous streak full of hatred and vitriolic bile. I hated the way she always spoke disparagingly of my father, insisting that I have nothing to do with him as he was so awful. I loved my father; I thought he was marvellous and devastatingly handsome too. My mother did all she could to freeze him out.

I knew she was fibbing about wanting more children too. I had sort of hoped that she might have a child by Stefan so I could help her look after it and we would have something of our own to love. However, one day when she was out and I was snooping at her lovely things like some sort of demented fan stalking a movie star, rummaging through her delicious-smelling face creams with exotic names like Douceline and Absolue Nuit; suddenly in the bottom drawer of her dressing table I found some contraceptive jelly in a tube and also an alarmingly weird cervical cap. The full instructions were still in the packet and I read with great interest but gutting disappointment, realising that there never would be a baby after all.

One cold afternoon early in the Christmas holidays of 1972, I was walking aimlessly along Kensington High Street when I bumped into a beautiful girl called Olga who I had admired from a distance, ever since I was a child, whenever I saw her at the Polish Club. She was wearing a mink coat and seemed to me the very essence of glamour. She was much remarked upon in Polish circles for having appeared in various publications and she was frequently mentioned in the gossip columns as a 'party girl'. She was much disapproved of but I found her so excitingly naughty. Olga had a beautiful face framed by glorious red-gold hair (obviously dyed, but who cares). She got various jobs as a photographic model due to her prettiness but she was very short, only five foot, so could not enter the big league of successful models. She tried to compensate for her lack of height by wearing very high stiletto heels and could often be seen tottering about with her short skirts, her red backcombed hair piled high. Her mother was a cabaret singer with over-bleached hair who wore jangling jewellery from Woolworths and flashy clothes. I had seen her once dressed in a whooshing, noisy full-skirted low-cut dress, over which she wore a huge fur coat and a hat with feathers clasped on with a brightly jewelled hat pin. She was held in very low esteem by the ultra-formal Polish community and never invited to elegant events. I had observed how the women froze and pursed their lips with disapproval in her presence when she entered the dining room of the Polish Club and the men would snigger and say things like 'here comes the Christmas tree' but she seemed impervious to criticism as she smiled and flirted.

I shyly approached Olga and she seemed happy to see me. She asked me to keep her company as a friend had stood her up for lunch and upon hearing that I had just turned fourteen she took me into Barkers department store and bought me a load of make-up as a present. Then we sat and had tea and she spoke openly of her life and how many boyfriends she had and asked me whether I had a boyfriend. She told me I could come with her to a coffee bar opposite Harrods at 5 p.m. as she was meeting a couple of young men and I readily agreed as I was lost and desperate. She told me to lie about my age and pretend I was seventeen. I knew that she had a reputation but she was kind to me and I found her thrilling.

We met the boys, Edward and Nick. They were both twenty-three-year-old law students and I found them thrilling as well with their impeccable manners. They stood up when we approached their table and greeted me with a warm handshake. They were jocular and bandied sophisticated witticisms, teasing Olga about her hair as she wore it so very backcombed but she laughed them off with a sort of peevish, pouting charm. I sat nervously, hoping neither of these handsome men would notice my bitten fingernails and listened entranced, saying little except that I was at school doing my A-level retakes; a wicked lie but most necessary under the circumstances and they believed me.

Then they even all suggested that I come to a party on Saturday. I needed little persuading. After a couple of hours of cheerful conversation we all parted with a kiss on the cheek and I dashed home to tell my mother, who immediately said I must wear her red Cheongsam dress which she would alter to fit me. That is just what I wanted, as she had looked fabulous in it but couldn't be seen in it again as she had already worn it a couple of times and people noticed that sort of thing.

Olga and her date, who had an E-Type Jaguar, came to pick me up at 7 p.m. on Saturday and I squeezed into the back, absolutely terrified. I rang my granny to tell her I was going to my very first grown-up party and she insisted I eat a hard-boiled egg and swallow a cod liver oil pill before drinking any alcohol as this would soak up the wine like blotting paper and I would not get drunk. Wise words and I still follow her rule to this day as it works a treat.

I was so excited I don't remember where the party was but it was a fine house with twinkling lights on the porch and lively Abba music inside. It was already crowded and we went upstairs to place our coats, trying to find a bedroom where there wasn't a couple on the bed snogging. 'Sorry, sorry,' we said as we went to another room. This made us laugh and lightened my nerves. When we walked in to the main room I was trembling and speechless with shyness so I stood hugging the wall. My dress seemed much admired and totally different to anyone else's and immediately I was asked to dance by a handsome chap. Olga gave me a little shove and said 'go on'. I adored her; she was like a fairy godmother, big sister and favourite aunt all rolled into one. Edward and Nick made me peal with laughter as when we were standing making cheerful conversation, Nick started putting little cocktail sticks into Olga's hair while she had her back to us talking to someone else. He must have placed about twenty, all of which stayed firmly put in hedgehog fashion, and from behind she looked very funny but did not have a clue why people were laughing all around and sniggering at her. 'Oh do stop it,' I said to Nick, feeling very loyal to my new best friend. I wanted to warn her of what was happening but when I tried to get her attention, Nick mischievously stopped me, saying, 'don't you dare.' The two of them always mocked Olga, regarding her as vacuous and silly, and never invited her along to more prestigious occasions; she had led me to the gates of high society but was unable to follow me across the threshold.

Thereafter, during the Christmas holidays I had a wonderful time and felt I had struck incredibly lucky. There were constant parties and dinners at San Lorenzo, usually in a large group of eight. And then on to Tramp nightclub in Jermyn Street. I was accepted as one of the crowd without question. It helped that I formed an attachment to Edward; he was a law student, as were a number of his friends, mostly Old Etonians, future lords and aspiring politicians and their girlfriends. They were united with a singular purpose of enjoying life, sharing the latest jokes, cultivating their wittiness and sarcasm. I soon felt comfortable in such sophisticated company and almost forgot my family troubles. I copied the older girls' mannerisms and plunged into a routine whirlwind of pleasure, starting with Saturday afternoons watching Edward and Nick playing tennis at Queen's Club. After they had finished playing they would go shower and change and a group of us would sit in the bar on comfy chairs where I would drink gin and orange whilst they cracked jokes. Then we would go to dinner somewhere fashionable like Meridiana in Fulham Road or San Lorenzo, though the owner, the great matriarch Mara Berni, would be awfully bossy, running her empire like a tight ship; woe betide anyone who was late for the early sitting at 8 p.m. The next sitting was at 10:30 p.m. but standing around at the bar waiting was like a huge, friendly cocktail party and there were few complaints. No one would dare complain about anything to Mara. She was short and plump and sharp-eyed with wisdom. She would ask about our lives and well-being and we all loved her in a respectful way. My favourite meal was the veal *melanzane alla parmigiana*. All visiting film stars and anyone of any social standing wouldn't dream of eating anywhere else and there was always a photographer outside.

I became a vibrant success in what I had previously thought an impenetrable social circle. I felt I had well and truly arrived and that my future was assured. Hunt balls in Wiltshire and house parties in Gloucestershire. However, upper-class weekend house parties were steamy with seduction and any pretty woman accepting an invitation needed to have her wits about her to deal with unwelcome tapping on her bedroom door at night from gentlemen with dishonourable intentions. Sadly, gentle rapes have frequently occurred.

When it was eventually time to get married I would only settle for a title, preferably a duke. Blimey, I thought, I might even get to marry the Prince of Wales at this rate. All the girls in my class at school had a crush on him and in the class above and the class below. Everyone in those days had the hots for Prince Charles. I even jokingly mentioned it to my grandfather, who looked at me quite sternly and told me not to be so silly; Prince Charles would never consider marrying a Polish girl, he would choose someone from his own kind and I was to choose from my own kind also. I was well aware that my father came from an aristocratic family well-documented as going back for hundreds of years and had a title of his own. He did not use it in England as he told me it was bad form to give yourself airs and graces when you are in someone else's country. Often I was teased for being Polish and once I replied to Nick's snobbish girlfriend Kate that, 'whilst it is true that I am Polish, I am of excellent pedigree.' She replied that that was a contradiction in terms and I felt a bit miffed but laughed it off.

In the meantime Edward would do. I had at first fancied Nick but decided he had a slightly cruel, superficial streak, being far too confident and handsome. I had my very first kiss with him in his car after we had spent the evening at the trendy Windsor Castle pub in Notting Hill but as I wouldn't let him put his hand up my jumper, he became peevish, so we parted company and he did not ring me the next day. I was a little bit upset but when I next saw him at Queen's Club he was amiable and teased me for being a schoolgirl still and the friendship continued. That is when he started going out with a twenty-two-year-old sexually experienced girl called Kate. And I know that she had the reputation of being one of the girls 'who did'. Far too liberal, I thought to myself.

I settled for Edward who was amusing, full of casual bravado and seemed much taken by me. He was a good-natured, reliable fellow of medium height with good teeth and dark, wavy hair. He dressed with an air of careless elegance but impeccably as a classic Sloane, sometimes in a three-piece suit, Chelsea boots and carrying a furled umbrella which he would wave at taxis. He lived with his parents in Harrington Gardens but I never met them, although whenever I rang Edward his mother was very charming to me on the phone.

Frequently I would let him in my upstairs door and we would spend happy evenings watching television and snogging, which I didn't mind just as long as he didn't stick his tongue in my mouth, I was never one for exchanging saliva and on the whole found too much bodily contact rather awful. He didn't have wandering hands and we got on well. He taught me how to play poker and often Nick would join us with Kate and we played for hours, though no money was exchanged. It was just for fun and to see who could win the most matchsticks. If my mother and Stefan were away in Devon or on the continent, we could all go down to the kitchen and make ourselves some cheese on toast and then take it back upstairs where we would wash it down with gin and tonic. But one evening when they were in London Stefan must have smelt too much cigarette smoke and he lurched into my room drunk and swaying and ordered Edward out. None of my friends were welcome.

Mum and Stefan often went to the South of France or to Spain and left me alone at home. Wooden shutters boarded up the front windows for security and they trusted me even at such a young age to be sensible. Also Misia lived quietly in the spare bedroom. I was perfectly responsible regarding my personal visitors and respected the position I was in of guarding the house. Very rarely, when I really wanted to show off to someone new, usually a friend of Edward's, I would lead them into Stefan's sitting room and switch on the six switches with dramatic aplomb so the lights came on all at once for maximum effect and my friends could see the splendour of the furnishings. But I never allowed anyone to touch anything or sit down and make themselves at home. They would admire the riches and then we would go upstairs again to my room. Occasionally I would allow my close friends Alistair and Caroline, who were in love and had nowhere else to go, to stay the night and they would occupy my mother's bedroom. But there was always the ghastly possibility of Mum and Stefan returning home unexpectedly and I did not take such risks too often.

No one tried to seduce me; it was accepted that good girls didn't and that was that. They accepted I was a virgin and there was much good-natured teasing about it. I retained an unassailable morality and besides no one had yet realised how young I was. There was another very prim and virtuous girl at Queen's Club called Virginia and the boys used to joke about her name saying, 'Virgin for short, but not for long!'

It was a great inconvenience to drag myself away from all this frivolity and return to boarding school where I was thought to be studying History and English Literature A-levels but Edward wrote regularly and sent me cigarettes which impressed the other girls, even though we couldn't smoke them as the nuns could detect the smell of smoke from miles away.

I left the hated convent aged sixteen and a half without even bidding the teachers farewell. Edward had a swanky car by now and he came to help me with my trunk. At the convent gates I gave my boater hat to a small foreign depressed new boarder as a present. I had achieved a handful of O-levels with excellent grades in English Language, Literature and History after applying myself to my studies and cramming for a few nights in a row. My mother had given me some amphetamine pills from the chemist to keep me awake and alert. They are totally illegal these days, as are the Nembutal pills which she gave me to get to sleep when I wanted. Nembutal is a deadly drug and frequently used by people of fashion as the drug of reliable choice to commit suicide. I read later that both Marilyn Monroe and Stephen Ward died from Nembutal overdoses. No one had such a trendy mum as mine.

After I left school I felt that I had shot myself in the foot as I had nothing to do. I could have gone to a tutorial crammer to do my A-levels but felt that, as I had been lying all the time that I had already done them twice, I couldn't get away with that excuse again. I would have felt hideously ashamed if anyone had discovered my true age.

I spent a pleasant summer with the ever-attentive Edward. We partied, we went to balls at the Dorchester Hotel and I remember once dancing for hours and leaving so late that the next day's newspapers were already on sale in Park Lane when we left at 3 a.m. I felt very grand walking along in my ball gown with a bevy of admirers. My confidence grew and it seemed that every boy or man I met fancied me. All the boys had E-Type Jaguars for a while but the rage for them soon passed as they all seemed to misjudge the length of bonnet and crash them, which then became a joke. Aston Martins were everywhere and one boy called James I went out with, in secrecy from Edward, had a Corvette Stingray, but I thought that was dreadfully vulgar. Edward even talked of marriage, thinking I was nineteen years old, so that took some wriggling out of. Despite warning me to stay away from Olga, my mother was pleased that I had fallen in with such good company and always made sure I was beautifully turned out in evening dresses, my favourite one being silvery pale-pink chiffon, not at all tight with a chiffon train. I looked marvellous and got my picture in *Tatler*.

I got a job in Harrods in the book department, which I loved. With my first week's wages I bought my mother a new clock radio, so she could keep it by her bed, and a new dress for myself. My mother told me not to let Stefan know about the dress; now that I was earning money of my own he would insist that I pay him for my keep and 'stop being such a parasite'.

One day I was passing an antique shop and saw in the window a tiny, exquisitely carved ivory elephant with his trunk held up high. It was such a pretty little thing, so I bought it for myself but as soon as I showed it to my mother she suggested to my horror that I give it to Stefan as a present. 'But I don't want to,' I replied, 'I love it and want to keep it for myself in my room.' She nagged and explained how this would please Stefan and make her life easier so I begrudgingly gave it to him. He had more antiquities than he knew what to do with and yet placed it in a cabinet that was already bursting with Meissen china and all manner of statuettes.

By the time I was seventeen and a half I decided that I really ought to give this sex thing a try, as I was fed up of everyone talking about it. I certainly wasn't going to compromise my reputation in London and risk the chance of not succeeding in a 'top drawer' marriage. Therefore I decided that I would get away from Stefan and my increasingly silly and nervous mother and go to Spain to lose my virginity. I caught a train to Alicante, having changed stations in Paris from the Gard de Lyon to the Gard du Nord (or the other way around) while managing not to get lost. Looking back, it seems like a miracle but I had the arrogant confidence of youth. I finally arrived at a pretty little town called Javea on the Costa Blanca near Benidorm, the latter being a joke with skyscraper hotels.

Mother Anguish

It was March and therefore out of season and the weather was mild. I found a boarding house run by a respectable family who gave me a room on the ground floor. I remember it was on the Calle de la Palma; road of the palm trees. Each morning I would wake early and walk straight to the market, where I bought a fresh crusty roll, still hot from the oven, along with two huge tomatoes and a bottle of San Miguel beer. Then I would go back to the boarding house and sit on my bed and munch it all up together and it was the most delicious breakfast ever. After that I would go to the beach and bake myself to a crisp and swim. Late afternoon I returned to my room to wash my hair, eat the other tomato and dress in something floaty or a pair of jeans and T-shirt, before going to the local shops on the main road to buy a copy of the *Daily Mail* and settle happily in a sidewalk bar. I soon made friends amongst the English ex-pats and also got to know a wonderful Spanish man called Jaime who took me home one day to meet his wife and eight children. His wife gave me some delicious lentil stew, the taste of which I have never forgotten, and insisted I come back for lunch the next day and the day after. They must have thought I was terribly young to be away from home all alone and were obviously perceptive enough to work out that I had some sort of troubles in England and decided to look after me.

I wanted to return home after a month but still hadn't found a suitable candidate for my de-flowering. I was also running out of money. I couldn't afford any Ambre Solaire and being quite sallow skinned I was already as brown as I wished to be, my stomach being almost black. One balmy evening I was sitting with some English people in a bar and I noticed an extremely handsome fellow observing me intently. He was swarthy, slim and muscular with very thick, curly, dark hair and fabulous teeth which showed whenever he flashed a smile in my direction. He soon inveigled himself into our group and laughed appreciatively at everything I said. His name was Graham and he told me he was twenty-nine years old, Australian and travelling the world in a campervan with his friend Paul. Everything about him was appealing, except that he never bought a round of drinks but he explained that he was very poor and doing Europe on the cheap.

Later that evening he asked me to go for a drink with him alone elsewhere. On the way he first popped into another bar and told me to wait a minute outside. I didn't feel like waiting and so naughtily followed him in and stood right behind him as he spoke to a very pretty girl working behind the bar and heard him breaking off a date which they had arranged for after she had finished her shift. She saw me standing there over his shoulder and I don't think I had ever seen such a look of naked jealousy and hatred on anyone's face as when she realised she was being dumped. Graham was cheerful womaniser, but that was normal. He told me that he had had his eye on me for a couple of weeks having observed me walking through the town and he always associated me with the song 'The Girl from Ipanema'.

He didn't try to kiss me that first evening and I was friendly but glamorously aloof. We parted with the plan that we would meet at an appointed place on the beach the next day. He amused me by climbing every palm tree he saw and he was a diverting change from the Hooray Henrys I knew so well in London. I was much impressed by his swimming too. I just wished he didn't often embarrass me in front of my English friends, having on one occasion asked someone to buy him a steak sandwich, the cost of which he didn't contribute to. He told me that when he was going out with the girl from the bar, she would feed him for free.

One night, being well fortified with Cinzano Bianco and in a spirit of curiosity and compassion as he was so broke, I had sex for the first time in his campervan, parked in a discreet spot out of town behind some trees. As the saying goes, I gave myself lightly, wantonly and ill-advisedly. It was OK, but no big deal. I couldn't understand what all the fuss was about and was certainly in no hurry to do it again; it hurt a bit so I was reluctant to repeat it for at least the next week. However, I felt truly grown-up and an ultra-sophisticated woman. And more to the point, no one need know; I would still marry well and get my large house near Sloane Square and stately pile in the country, with horses and a big dog and a little dog, and hopefully a holiday house in Cap Ferrat.

Graham was always mentioning how broke he was and his parents disapproved of him being in Europe as they had never even been out of Melbourne. They bombarded him with letters to the local *poste restante*, ordering him home but he had an adventurous spirit and wanted to follow me to London. The plan was that having seen Big Ben and Madame Tussauds, he would return from whence he came from in the glorious Antipodes. My mother sent me money for my air fare home but I gave some to Graham as he didn't have enough for the petrol and we decided to drive through Spain en route to London and stop and see Madrid too. He irritated me a bit in Madrid as one afternoon I was feeling famished, so asked him for some of my money back as I wanted to buy something to eat but he refused saying he needed it for the petrol. However I noticed that he was still buying cigarettes for himself.

We eventually arrived in London in the middle of the night and upon reaching Elvaston Place I called my mother's name loudly from the dark quiet street: 'Mummy, Mummy, I'm home!' It was about 3 or 4 a.m. and I was overjoyed to see my home again before my mother's face appeared at the window telling me to shush in case I woke Stefan. I dare say I woke all the neighbours but it was so good to be in beloved London that I didn't care. Graham parked his van in Elvaston Mews and slept in it.

My mother let me in, made me some food and mentioned that my breasts had got bigger. She asked me when my period was due and I realised then that I was two weeks late. From feeling so grown-up and sophisticated, I suddenly felt full of very childlike dismay and horror. I was pregnant.

Chapter 5

My mother was remarkably calm and we decided not to panic as it was still early days and my periods were irregular. She rummaged around in her cupboard and gave me two pills to swallow called Amenorone Forte, which she said would bring on my period and which I've since discovered contained a massive dose of oestrogen. It didn't work and the following week we made an appointment with a doctor of her choosing. I am sure she had plenty of experience regarding abortions and I was entirely guided by her but I didn't like the doctor who performed a perfunctory examination on me in his consulting room; situated in a block above Baker Street station, of all places. He advised waiting another month as terminations were more successful when there was more substance inside and there wasn't a risk of missing anything. Needless to say, these were the days before the morning-after pill or early vacuum aspiration.

So I went back to work at Harrods, not concentrating at all and greatly disturbed by the little life growing inside me. I told Graham but he was flabbergasted and disbelieving and didn't really want to talk about it as it was all just too much for him. I saw him every day as he was still living and sleeping in the campervan in Elvaston Mews. It was a funny arrangement; when Stefan was out I would let Graham into the house through my private entrance on the second floor so that he could have a bath and shave and for the rest of the time he explored London, or lay around in Hyde Park while I worked at Harrods. He had no money but had travelled from Australia with about fifty boomerangs which he laid out on the grass in Hyde Park and tried to sell. However, he was soon moved on by the authorities as all commercial exchanges are forbidden in the park. I sneaked him into my room in the evening to watch television and then he would leave and sleep in the van.

I quickly consulted my friend Olga about my predicament, swearing her to secrecy. She said she had had two abortions already. She also told me it was early days so I should try drinking half a bottle of gin before taking a hot bath and sticking tweezers up my nose to pull the little hairs in an attempt to bring on severe sneezing fits. I tried all of this plus every other old wives' tale I'd heard, including swallowing packets of laxatives, carrying heavy piles of books and jumping off the kitchen table. I also went to a gym which had a wide vibrating belt machine on which women would press their bottoms and savagely pound away their cellulite. I stood the other way around with my stomach receiving the violent vibrations. But my pregnancy stuck fast and I tried to lead life as normally as I could under the circumstances.

Graham was becoming quite a liability. I was fond of him but it had been a holiday romance involving beaches, palm trees and bars; a stark contrast to cosmopolitan London. My mother took pity on him because he was so thin and poor, so it became a habit that he would come to my room each evening and Mother would bring us up two plates of food without Stefan's knowledge. She fed him a fine dinner every day and he was very grateful and seemed almost infatuated with her. My friends mocked me for taking up with an ocker Aussie and those that I introduced him to found his conversation banal and simplistic. He was way out of his league when they talked of politics, law or the stock markets. My friends laughed themselves silly when they saw his Volkswagen camper-van, which had a big map of Australia painted on both sides. They thought he was awful and he thought they were terrible snobs. At times I felt dreadfully sorry for him trying to fit in to the hur-ly-burly of London life, although he was terribly arrogant and kept telling me my friends were boring and stuck-up. He criticised everything. I really wanted him to enjoy London but we had a hideously embarrassing moment when he said he wanted to go to the Rib Room of the Carlton Tower hotel in Sloane Street but they wouldn't let him in as he wasn't wearing a tie. After that I was far too ashamed to risk taking him to Queen's Club. But to do him justice, he did the honourable thing and stayed in London until my pregnancy problem was resolved. At that time marriage to Graham was out of the question because we were from different worlds and different cultures.

On the appointed day of my abortion, I went early in the morning with my mother to the room above Baker Street station. The doctor had another man there, probably just another professional abortionist, but they were short, squat and middle-aged and I felt uncomfortable and freaked out, desperate not to lie down there on the couch in that dingy brown room. I was so terrified, I started to cry. I told my mother I couldn't go through with it and then ran away.

A few days later my mother took me see another doctor in Harley Street, a Dr Rosenberg, who agreed to do it the following Tuesday in a clinic in St John's Wood, under general anaesthetic.

I approached the clinic, which was in a very pretty house, on that sunny Tuesday in August feeling in a better frame of mind and desperate to have the problem put behind me; although I was being realistic, expecting all sorts of unpleasant probabilities and wished I had never set eyes on Graham.

The surgery was done and my most vivid recollection was when a nurse came to my room to change my dressings later that evening. There I lay, half propped up on the bed, watching her pull out wads and wads of blood-soaked gauze from between my legs using a metal instrument. I stared wordlessly at this terrible spectacle and I remember the radio ironically playing a song with the lyrics, 'too late to worry, too late to change your mind,' sung to such a pretty tune. I stayed the night and the next day my mother picked me up by taxi to take me home.

Mother Anguish

About ten days later, I realised I hadn't been feeling well for some time and had painful stomach cramps but Graham wanted to take me to the park. As I was getting dressed, I felt something fall out of me and on to the carpet. I picked it up and scrutinised it and saw it was a chunk of a tiny ribcage about the size of a grape, pale and rotten and stinking of putrefaction. I immediately went to my mother next door, who recoiled in horror upon smelling it and rang Dr Rosenberg straight away. He told her to bring me to his surgery after hours that night somewhere off the Earls Court Road and to tell no one. We went at 8 p.m. not knowing what to expect. He looked very serious, not as twinkly as before, and there was a very old and thin little woman there in white uniform as well. I lay on his couch for an examination and she held my hand tightly as he proceeded to tell me to be brave. He explained that the last time had been an incomplete evacuation, meaning that part of the foetus had been left behind to decompose inside me; he would have to repeat the procedure all over again but without anaesthetic as he had none there. To this day it is a mystery to me why it all had to be done after hours and in secret. Why hadn't he sent an ambulance for me earlier in the day and had me admitted into a hospital, or the clinic at least?

When it was all over, my mother and I took a taxi home and she put me to bed and gave me a small alcoholic drink, saying we must drink to the future; she was very calm and pragmatic. The doctor gave me two massive bottles of the strongest antibiotics and I was told to stay in bed because I was septic inside. He sternly instructed my mother to contact him immediately if my condition worsened as my temperature was high. I don't remember much else but he visited me daily and when I was feeling a bit better I asked the question on my mind; whether because of this infection I might never have children in the future. He smiled at me kindly and stroked my forehead, saying, 'of course you will have children and I will stand as their godfather,' but I didn't believe him and I cried with terror that I had murdered a little human being and also, as a punishment, had destroyed any chance of a decent future for myself. I was terrified that I would never be able to have a family of my own.

From that moment on, my psychological state was so deranged that all I could think about was my desperation to have a baby, just to see if I was irreparably damaged inside. There was no counselling or reading matter to reassure me in those days and my mother and I never spoke of it at all. But it hung heavily on my mind and I was tormented with fear and guilt and consumed by my anxiety-ridden thoughts. I peered into every pram I saw and my heart ached. My friend Olga, on the other hand, had gossiped about my misfortune to absolutely everybody. I found out from Nick's spiteful girlfriend Kate a short time after, as I had drifted apart from my social circle over the last few weeks because of my involvement with Graham and their mutual dislike. I went to Olga's flat in Baron's Court, a ghastly part of town and, sitting on her bed, asked her why she had to tell Kate and Nick about my abortion but she just shrugged her shoulders and said 'sorry' and admitted to everything. I didn't stay long and refused her offer of a cup of tea. She was too self-absorbed to care about the damage she had done and I was furious to see my good name thoughtlessly dragged through the mud.

I have always found a certain irony in the fact that my descent to hell was precipitated by a foolish sexual encounter, as I generally consider sex to be one of life's most overrated pleasures, save for when one is madly in love. I knew then that I could never make a splendid marriage in England, as high-status boys wanted virgins, or at least girls who hadn't been talked about. My erstwhile boy-friend Edward was so angry and heartbroken that I'd taken up with Graham that after hearing about my subsequent calamity he was going around London saying, 'I'm going to beat the little bugger up,' although Graham was in fact significantly taller than him. I was much gossiped about and found all of it so difficult to cope with that I decided that I must leave England in shame and marry elsewhere and have the baby I was desperate for, if only to prove that I could. It may seem irrational now but I was only a teenager at the time and in shock and I could see no end to my humiliating fall from grace at the hands of Olga and the rumour mill. I was gripped by a desire to run away and decided to join Graham in heading back to the Antipodes and return at a later date with a child. My mother paid for my one-way ticket to Australia and gave me £40 in cash to tide me over. All this drama had been too much for her I think and having a wayward daughter at home was an inconvenience and damaging to her marriage with Stefan.

The day before I left I went to Queen's Club and despite my friends' warnings, kept up the pretence of exuberance appropriate for someone setting off on a long trip to see the world. All my friends told me I was mad but, despite my fears, I did feel somewhat like a pioneer embarking on an adventure. Who knew what adventures and exotic sights lay before me? One much older man, who had never spoken to me before, came up to me and shook my hand and sincerely wished me 'good luck'. Obviously he knew my story too and I felt as though I was going to my execution. That night, alone in my room, I watched a series on television and realised sombrely that this time next week I wouldn't be there to see what happened in the next episode. In those days emigrating to Australia was tantamount to death. Earlier that day my poor grandparents came to Elvaston Place to bid me goodbye. With tears streaming down their dignified faces, they blessed me, making the sign of the cross on my forehead and when they left I sadly watched them from my window as they walked away down the road, two dreadfully unhappy old people. I felt so guilty for recklessly disregarding their feelings; all my life they had been so kind to me and now I was abandoning them in their old age.

On the day of my departure, I came down to the kitchen early with my mother but Stefan was not there. He must have got up at the crack of dawn and left the house. He didn't return for lunch or in the afternoon, so we never said goodbye and my mother and I were both puzzled by his behaviour. It was never explained. In the evening my mother's friends Tomasz and Ursula drove me to the airport. It was a November night, rainy and dark, and as we sat in silence, all I could hear was the rain lashing down and the sound of my mother's weeping. I morosely looked out the window and bid farewell to England; goodbye for now but I would return soon I kept telling myself.

My mother made sure I had lots of beautiful clothes and I intended to cause a sensation in Melbourne, which after all was a one-horse town. Graham met me upon my arrival in the late morning and drove me home to see his mother, who was called Effie and lived in a suburb called East Malvern. Effie was fifty-two years old; a short, stout, pleasant woman with stocky legs, freshly permed bright lilac hair and obvious dentures that kept slipping. Benign and boring but harmless, I immediately thought. Graham's father was called Garnet and he and Effie had met in the same class at primary school, spent their entire lives living walking distance from each other and after they married they had remained in that area. They didn't believe in travel as Melbourne was the centre of the world to them. They had never even been to Sydney and had no desire to.

East Malvern was the third most exclusive suburb in Melbourne, ten miles from the city, the second one being South Yarra and the premier one being Toorak, which was full of glorious mansions nestled in gardens of at least one acre. Unfortunately Effie and Garnet were not in that sphere, so they built for themselves a house of Garnet's design in Thornberry Crescent. It was supposed to be a copy of an English house as one might have looked in Garnet's mind's eye and had leadlight windows, a high-pitched roof and an arched porch. Neither of them had seen an English house in real life, having never travelled, but it was very pretty indeed, although small; a cottage really and I was disappointed when I first saw it, especially as it was built opposite a railway line. Effie told me that Garnet, who was always very careful with his money, had bought that plot of land as it was cheaper than around the corner on the other side of the crescent, where a couple of the houses were two storey. One time I made the ghastly mistake of mischievously saying to Effie and Garnet that the origin of the word 'bungalow' was that once, long ago, some builders decided to build a house but ran out of bricks, so one builder said to the other 'Lets bung a low roof on'.

Effie's house had two bedrooms only; Graham and his brother Ian had shared one throughout their childhood and adulthood. And the entire house had just four rooms altogether. After twenty-five years of marriage Effie had persuaded Garnet to build a sunroom extension, where she kept her plants. The back garden was mostly covered in concrete as it was less trouble to maintain than flower beds; there were no flowers at all except for a magnolia tree at the very end and an ugly rotary hoist took pride of place in the middle of the back yard for Effie to hang her washing on. In front of the house stood a large silver birch tree but that was all, no flowers. When Effie asked me if it reminded me of England, I tried to be as complimentary as possible. All their windows had plastic venetian blinds operated by a chord that could be adjusted to let in as much or as little light as one wanted. Therefore curtains were not required but Effie had ten-inch-wide strips of fabric on either side of the windows 'just for show'. What manner of people are these, I thought, recalling my opulent home in London with its velvet armchairs, its brocade curtains with silken tie-backs and golden tassels. This was a far cry from the splendour of Knightsbridge and I wanted to go home.

Garnet and Effie's house was a solid brick structure, which was considered very prestigious, I was told, as most Australian houses were brick veneer only or weatherboard (slatted wood, painted white). Solid brick was very costly but stayed cooler in the scorching hot spells. That being said it retained the heat after the cool change came and Effie would open all the doors and windows to let in some air, welcoming a barrage of flies along with the breeze. Each window and doorway had a wire fly screen and the front door as well but betwixt opening one and the other as fast as one could, somehow the crafty flies managed to slip past and swarm into the house. Effie had fly swatters hanging in every room and I had never come across one before but for a while enjoyed the target practice; squashing flies on the wall was normal practice, after which one washed off the splotches.

The house had a sitting room which they called a lounge but it was never used unless there was company, which they never had, and a dining room in which they sat all the time as the television was in the corner. It was quite small and the dining table was always pushed under a window and then pulled out again for mealtimes and chairs re-arranged. Opposite were two armchairs where Effie would sit and knit and Garnet would smoke his pipe silently. Both sitting room and dining room had grey rose-patterned fitted carpet.

I looked around the house and found no decorative works of art, besides some prints which were hung by unsightly wires from picture rails near the ceiling as Garnet did not allow nails damaging the walls; Effie explained to me that Garnet disliked 'clutter'. To my horror there was not a single book in sight. Oooops, I thought, realising that these were the ultra-respectable lower middle class; untraveled, unsophisticated, uneducated, yet with pretentions of grandeur based on the ownership of a large car. Garnet owned a Studebaker; iridescent pale brown and as large as a Cadillac, it was his pride and joy and also his phallic symbol, I deduced. He polished it in the front of the house each Saturday, showing off to the neighbours. That was his chief joy. I was always of the opinion that people's personalities are expressed by their taste in furniture, art, clothes and amusements yet these people were totally unaware of world history and literature. Neither of them had ever read a book since leaving school and they never ever read the daily newspapers. Effie admitted that in her youth she had tried reading *Gone with the Wind* but couldn't finish it so she gave it away. I could scarcely conceal my incredulity. It was beyond the bounds of my comprehension that people could be so disinterested in culture and cultivation.

Garnet came home at the end of each day and we all sat down to a silent dinner (they called it 'tea') of roast lamb, pumpkin and peas cooked by Effie, which tasted very nice. I complimented her on the roast pumpkin, which I had never tasted before, doing my best to be very polite. Garnet was a good-looking man, an older version of Graham but very quiet. He rarely spoke and had a near-permanent expression of world-weariness and displeasure about him. He totally disapproved of travelling and kept repeating that you should 'see Australia first', though they had never been outside of Melbourne. I laughingly told them that Australia was but an island which thought it was a continent and there was a deathly silence. When I spoke of England, they were pompous, patronising and condescending and it soon became evident that they had been horrified to learn that I was Polish and didn't even know where Poland was. I once overheard Effie urging Graham to find himself 'a nice Australian girl'.

They were very refined and particular in their speech and always spoke delicately saying 'pardon' instead of 'what?' which they considered the height of ill breeding. At table they spoke of 'serviettes' and when I said 'napkin' Effie tut-tutted in disapproval as napkins were what you put on babies' bottoms. Having never met a formally educated English person before, they were horrified by my speech and insisted repeatedly that I spoke with a very heavy Polish accent. I explained that they were mistaken as I had been born and privately schooled in England and spoke the language correctly but they didn't agree and constantly told me, 'You have a very, very strong Polish accent, we can tell, we can tell,' nodding smugly. They were aghast at what they perceived as my foreign coarseness when I referred to a lavatory or a loo. 'One must always say "toilet",' Effie instructed primly and Graham backed her up and begged me to talk properly and stop putting him to shame.

I stayed with them for a couple of weeks, sleeping on a pallet in the sun room, and in that time learnt about the slow-paced Australian way of life. Effie cooked roast lamb and potatoes, pumpkin and peas every day and admittedly it was delicious. I could find no fault with her cooking and lovely gravy. Sometimes she did roast pork. There were no other culinary variations at all, except on Saturdays, when she would take it easy and everyone had Frankfurters with buttered crumpets, and Sundays, when for lunch she made a strawberry pavlova, which was Australia's national pudding. They were disapproving when I used the word 'pudding', saying that it was a very common way to talk and that one must always say 'dessert'. I replied that in the English upper classes one always calls it 'pudding', even if it is ice cream, and they gawped with disbelief.

Effie went to the shops on Mondays, respectably dressed, wearing a hat and white gloves and carrying a wicker basket. On Thursdays she went to the local bowling club and on Fridays she always went to the hairdressers for a 'wash and set', during which she would have her hair sprayed with lacquer until it was a rock-solid blue helmet. She was a calm woman and on a ledge in her kitchen she had a bottle of Valium from which she took three 5-mg doses a day. She never had any reason whatsoever to go to the city and confined her shopping to the local high street. She told me that she had not been to town for over ten years. I remember that if either of her sons asked their mother a question she would answer 'we'll see when Father gets home' and that was that. She was a totally subjugated housewife. She made no decisions of any kind.

Graham's father Garnet was a remarkably curious character; he was seemingly near mute and when eating he would chew his mouthfuls of food for many more minutes than was necessary before swallowing. Effie seemed a little intimidated by him and hardly any conversation flowed at the dinner table as they watched the television. They knew nothing of politics or world affairs as they were not at all interested in the news from abroad. If anyone did speak to Garnet, he would continue chewing his food and stare at the wall and one was never quite sure whether he had heard. Eventually after an uncomfortable silence he would answer monosyllabically and then with no humour and intellect. Garnet had inherited a printing business in the city with about twenty staff from his father Fred who had died of drink. It was called Modern Reproduction, which I joked sounded like an obstetrics clinic but no one found it funny and Graham reprimanded me for being cheeky. He fancied himself as a bit of a dominant male family tyrant. Occasionally if Graham got home first and parked his car in the driveway, Garnet would follow later and deliberately block him in instead of parking in front of the house. Many a time I heard Graham ask his dad to please move his car after dinner so that he could drive his own out but Garnet would completely ignore his requests, staring into space and chewing the remains of his pudding.

Graham and Ian still lived at home aged twenty-nine and twenty-six respectively. Ian was as blond as Graham was dark and twice as stupid, with a vacant expression and constantly bloodshot eyes from swimming. He admitted that 'books were boring' and educating girls was a waste of time and money. He told me that when he was to get married, he wanted his wife to cook and be a good 'homemaker'. His only passion was surfing and he had a large surfboard with 'shark bait' printed on the side. He was also part of the 'Life-savers Association' and attended constant drills, marching along the seashore. I am sure he would have been capable of a rescue in a case of drowning but the opportunity never presented itself.

The Christmas holidays were soon upon us and it was at this time that Effie and Garnet went to the annual Photo Engravers

Dinner Dance, their one real night out of the year as they never even went to restaurants or the cinema. We all had a traditional Christmas dinner together with the venetian blinds closed against the oppressive heat of a bright, sweltering summer's day. There was an enormous turkey and trimmings and into the Christmas pudding Effie had mixed a handful of small three-penny silver coins, as to find one in your mouth was supposed to bring traditional good luck. I ate very carefully in case I broke a tooth or choked to death.

They didn't have any friends that I ever saw and never travelled anywhere except for the Lakes Entrance area in East Gippsland, which was four hours' drive away by an inland sea; there they had a primitive holiday home surrounded by ghastly caravan sites with no shops where we all stayed for a few days after Christmas. It had no garden at all as trees would be a danger in case of bushfires, and Garnet mowed the grass as low as possible as that could catch fire as well. I heard of many tragic stories of poor people fleeing for their lives along flat country roads but still getting burnt alive in their cars as the surrounding grass caught fire. There was a beach but the water was very shallow and full of jellyfish. I was very alarmed when warned of blue-ringed octopuses, which were commonly found in crevices and shallow rock pools throughout Australian coastal waters. These creatures have a yellowish-brown body ringed by blue stripes and their tentacles span only 3-4 inches. Their bite is almost painless but the venom released is absolutely lethal; full-body cessation of muscle activity is soon induced and death occurs through respiratory failure very quickly. If you are bitten, there is no point in even trying to get to the hospital as you won't make it. It is much worse in Queensland, I was told, where the stonefish is found all along the coast. It is not easily recognised, appearing just like any other stone and only moving when disturbed. A human foot or hand placed on it is likely to be pierced by one of the fish's dorsal spines and injected with its deadly venom. The immediate result is unbearable pain and the victim collapses almost at once.

Mother Anguish

This country is not for me, I decided; if one survives the spiders, hornets and sharks and other killer things in the water, one then risks being burnt to death in a bush fire.

It was awful and after experiencing that life for two weeks I was quite ready to return home and go to Harrods but realised I had to stick it out for a bit. I was very aware that I had entered Melbourne by the back door and that these people were not of elevated, intelligent society. It was indeed social amputation for me. I was suffering transportation for my crime but I kept telling myself that when I had served my time I would return to my homeland in triumph. I often laughed with an attitude of despair and frustration but I held beneath a determination that I would survive.

Graham introduced me to his friends at an evening party a few days after I arrived. Effie said they had all heard of me and were keen to look me over. Graham's friends were all around his age, twelve years older than me, and mostly married. The men cheerfully fetched me drinks but there were a few desperate single girls who regarded me with resentment and suspicion, conscious of being 'left on the shelf' and all but the very ugliest had been previous discarded girlfriends of Graham's. They were all callously cool as they scrutinised me from top to toe. I was dressed in a white lacy top and skirt with stockings and high-heeled shoes. Graham later said to me that he had never been so embarrassed in his life, as all the other girls wore shorts and had long bronzed oiled legs with their bare feet in thongs. But how was I to know the dress code. Whenever they did speak to me they would unsmilingly ask how long was I planning to stay in Melbourne and wasn't I homesick for my parents? They all said that England was going to the dogs and was full of foreigners and black people. Australia was God's own country; 'The Lucky Country', they called it.

I like to think I treated them with elegant, withering politeness and that my aristocratic genetic structure had bred into me a charming condescension inherited from generations of the grandest ancestors. I developed a look of tolerant superiority and disdain for their spite. You will never get the better of me, I thought with amused contempt, because I am different from other people, I have it in my DNA, it is in my blood; whereas you are all descended from England's failures, the lowest classes and dregs of society, England's outcasts, not to mention the criminal class. Nobody leaves a happy home and a successful life and none of England's exclusive people would have ever dreamt of emigrating while they flourished in their own country.

I decided I wanted to live by myself and rented a tiny one-bedroom flat in a suburb called Glen Iris. It was in a small block with a flat roof and I lived on the first floor. My door was on the landing, which was accessible from the street so I felt a bit unsafe but otherwise I thrived on my solitude and a freedom that I had never known before. With no one to obey, I could eat and sleep when I chose. I furnished it with a few bits I picked up from junk shops and got a book on French polishing. It appealed to me to refurbish the old pieces I bought and I busied myself with little wads of shellac, wet and dry sandpaper and turpentine and felt very artistic. The flat was bright and faced the afternoon sun so it got very hot but the large windows were covered with venetian blinds. It seemed that every window in every house in Melbourne had plastic venetian blinds. I wondered if it was the same in the lovely suburb of Toorak but didn't know anyone who even knew of anyone who lived there. We were worlds apart. I had stupidly fallen in with a bunch of muppets I decided. What is funnier still is that on occasions when Graham wanted to sneer at the people who lived there, he would always refer to them as 'bloody Toorakites'. He must have been consumed with jealousy, envy and begrudgery. All his friends were aware of their inferior status and boasted of the people they knew who lived in Toorak, though I never met any.

I realised that I had to get a job of some kind as I had rent to pay, but Effie and Garnet did not suggest anything or advise me.

Mother Anguish

They had no influential acquaintances who might have given me a leg up. In truth they expressed no personal interest in my welfare of any kind, although I was still a teenager without friends or family and therefore in danger of many perils. They did invite me for dinner once each week but otherwise I felt totally cast adrift and nervous living alone in my little flat. Graham would come over in the evenings and then go home.

I caught a number 6 tram to the city. Melbourne trams were coloured cream and green and had an open section in the middle for fresh air. The journey took over an hour and once there I applied to get a job in a big store called Myers. I sat in the personnel department all afternoon waiting for an interview. I told them I had worked in Harrods in London but they had never heard of it. However, it was successful nonetheless. They said they had vacancies in the handbag or book departments, so without hesitation I said 'books please' and there I was happily placed. I lied about my age, adding on ten years, as there was no way I wanted to work for a junior salary; I was so full of youthful confidence regarding my superior convent education and Latin O-level that I felt I could hold my own with any Australian. The manager didn't check and accepted me readily, complimented me on how young I looked and how fresh my complexion was.

Shortly after I arrived in Melbourne I fell ill with a kidney infection and having no medical insurance I ended up on a public ward of the general hospital for a week. It was an awful experience and Effie did not visit me once, though Graham did and I think he found it all very tiresome. Australia is full of southern-hemisphere viruses and germs that Europeans have no immunity to. As soon as I recovered, I returned to work and was kindly allowed to sit occasionally with a hot water bottle on my painful back as the management knew I had been ill. However, I never wrote of my health to my mother, playing down my unhappiness to soothe whatever anxieties she might have had about me being so far away.

Basia Briggs

The manager of the department, Mr Chamberlain, took rather a shine to me; too much of a shine actually. He was a rotund, dark-haired little man with licentious eyes. He often gazed at me and once I returned his stare mischievously. It was useful to have a gentleman admirer and thereafter he did not make a fuss or dock my pay if I was a little bit late, which was sometimes the case as the tram journey from Glen Iris could take ages. After working there for a few weeks, during which time I was encouraged to take a book home with me every night to be well informed on all subjects and able to advise customers, I felt very knowledgeable. Mr Chamberlain then asked me to come into his office for a chat, which I readily did, expecting to get an increase in wages. But instead of a pay rise, he pushed me against his desk and tried to grope and kiss me. I remember being so incensed that, seeing his hand lying flat down on the desk's surface, I picked up a pencil and stabbed it as hard as I could with the sharp point. He let go and I returned to my position on the shop floor rather nonchalantly, although my heart was pounding and my mouth was dry with shock and stress. Fifteen minutes later I was summoned to the personnel department by the store manager, who was a thin and severe middle-aged woman dressed in a stylish navy suit with an elegant broach on her lapel. I fully expected to get the sack. However, I did not. Sitting in her office full of outrage, I furiously explained how the man had dared to take such liberties and I shall never forget her words in response: 'He who angers you, conquers you.' She was an uncommonly wise and sensible woman and I treated her respectfully. With that I was informed I would be moved away from the book department where I had been so content and they placed me in the cosmetics department on the Revlon counter, which I tolerated but there is only so long one can play with lipsticks; it did not nourish my brain. Word got around the store that I had stabbed a senior member of staff and I was much amused that the men treated me with respect and kept their distance.

Mother Anguish

I started selling my pretty clothes for a fraction of their value to my workmates to raise the fare home. My mother wrote regularly, always including a £1 note, and I lived for her letters. I missed her dreadfully and I told her how homesick I was but she said Stefan wouldn't like it if I returned so soon and that it would be best for my reputation if I married Graham; if I returned to London now, she said, everyone would gossip that he had jilted me. To sweeten the idea she said she would come to Melbourne for my wedding.

When Graham unexpectedly announced to Garnet and Effie that we were getting married, the four of us were sitting at the dinner table. Effie went, 'Oooh,' but without much enthusiasm and Garnet completely ignored the announcement. He didn't say a word; he just continued chewing the strawberries he had been eating and staring into space and in the silence we could hear the little seeds being crunched. Graham and I waited and waited for some reaction from the man but there was none so he said, 'Come on Bash, let's go,' and we left. I found Garnet's reaction insulting.

I didn't like Australia; I considered the people pretentious philistines and incredibly racist, full of a hatred for Italians and Greeks which baffled me. They referred to Italians as 'wogs'. 'But the Italians are wonderful people,' I would say, 'they invented opera, they invented pizza.' My words were of little use, as they would never understand that the lowest-class Italian had more culture in his little finger than the average beer-guzzling Aussie had in their entire being. Effie told me of a petition being signed in her street, as word had got out that an Italian family wanted to buy a house there and all the other residents were determined to keep them out. They were convinced that if such foreigners moved into their area, it would lower the value of their own property. I thought it would be wonderful to have some Italian neighbours and hoped that perhaps they could teach me a bit more Italian vocabulary, as I had learnt a bit at school but was keen to speak the language better. I asked 'Why do you hate them?' and the response I got was unforgettable.

Effie said it was disgusting how the 'Ities' came to Australia and often brought their granny with them so that she could look after the babies while the adults all went out and worked extremely hard for very long hours. And then, she continued, when they had saved a lot of money, 'they would build themselves a really big house.' This was said with deadly seriousness and disapproval, with her lower lip quivering and her dentures wobbling and I shook my head with sad incomprehension. There was no point in trying to change Effie's mind as she didn't have the intellectual machinery. She and her type were the silliest class of snob, as they were so insecure that they have to look down on someone, anyone, just to feel better but didn't possess the graciousness of good breeding to be courteous to all and certainly not the dustman, I noticed.

I had met a few incredibly charming Australians in England at Queen's Club and came to the conclusion that all the decent Aussies were in England while the dregs remained back home swigging beer and throwing another shrimp on the barbie. Once when I was waiting for letters from England, which were the only scraps of connection to the outside world I had to keep me sane, I saw the postman stopping next door on his motorcycle and I approached him eagerly and said 'Hello, Mr Postman, are there any letters for me?' Effie said there is no need to use the prefix 'Mr' as he was only a 'service provider'.

If people like Graham's family come into contact with the rung below them, they perceive them as extremely vulgar and object if they copy any aspect of their lifestyle, such as buying a similar colour of car but when they meet someone who is a notch above them, such as those who live in South Yarra, then they succumb to toady grovelling. I would imagine that if they ever met anybody from Toorak they would pass out. These poor lower middle classes really are ridiculous, as they possess neither the grandeur and demeanour of the truly upper class nor the humour of the lower working class and therefore are despised by both. I pitied them with a bemused contempt and considered dwelling amongst them as a good anthropological study.

Australia was a class-ridden, illogical minefield of a society, with everyone, if the truth be told, feeling socially insecure but doing their best to hide it. Status anxiety, I think it is called. They all looked down on the English as well; in fact the lowest-class Australian still felt superior to the English migrant. I was repeatedly called a stuck-up, whinging pom whenever I commented on the Australian weather, not to mention the flies, and the spiders, some as big as your hand. 'Bloody well go back to where you came from if you don't like it here,' I was told by a friend of Graham's called Margot. She considered herself very grand as her father was a doctor.

I didn't like Graham's way of life either; the strong, bronzed Adonis I had met in Spain had turned into a slob with a beer gut. He drank beer like mother's milk and at parties all the men would stand around in the kitchen getting plastered while the girls were expected to sit in another room. There was no mixing at all. We drove to one such event, about twenty miles out in the Dandenong hills and I was made to feel so unwelcome by the tight clique of women that I wandered into the kitchen. But Graham just laughed at me in front of the lads. I went outside to sit in the car in the dark, listening to the high-pitched sound of mosquitoes buzzing around my head and after a long while Graham came out with a vegemite sandwich and couldn't understand why I was being so difficult. 'But the girls are so mean to me,' I told him in tears and he laughed. We stayed there until dawn and drove back to Melbourne in silence.

I resolved that I would marry him to save face and teach all those nasty girls a lesson; and then I would have the baby I wanted and return to London without further ado. That was the plan. He would do as a first husband/sperm donor and next time I would marry up. I would get someone of exalted status and no one need know the truth about the Australian bumpkins I had fallen in with.

Actually, the idea of divorce rather appealed to me, as my mother had been a divorcee and her mother in turn, so I associated it with great glamour.

My mother arrived by cruise ship and I wept with joy as I hugged her upon meeting at the docks. She was vivacious and vibrant, having enjoyed a month-long affair with the ship's captain, needless to say. She was beautifully dressed in a short cream-coloured Dior suit and she had brought a suitcase of new clothes for me as well. How I loved her.

Chapter 6

Graham and I drove her to my tiny flat in Glen Iris and it was terrible squash, especially as my mother had brought three trunkfuls of luggage. Graham was a great fan of my mother and I was pleased that they got on so well. My mother was in high spirits, as this had been her first taste of freedom since her marriage to Stefan six years previously. I think she went quite wild on the sea voyage and she told me that the captain had upgraded her to suite no. 2, his being suite no. 1, to facilitate their naughty sexual encounters. The photographs show that she sat at his table every night for dinner and I would imagine it was a very torrid and passionate voyage.

That evening Effie and Garnet came over. It was the first time they had ever ventured to my flat. We had hardly any room and I sat on the floor. Although they were very racist and whenever they referred to me being 'foreign' their voice had a certain tone, as if implying that I was not quite clean, they seemed charmed by my mother, who sparkled and did her best to put them under her spell. She was so glamorous; to Effie she must have seemed like a visitor from outer space. She certainly succeeded with Garnet, who had hardly shown any signs of life before and who I had almost never seen smile. Now he stared at her with boggle-eyed admiration, too tongue-tied to engage in intelligent conversation. She was beautifully dressed and her hands and wrists dazzled with jewels. Stefan had always bought her rubies and diamonds and she had quite a collection. I felt a bit sorry at Effie's discomfiture, as all she had apart from her wedding and engagement rings was a single string of Mikimoto pearls which Garnet bought her for their twentieth wedding anniversary and she never wore, saving them 'for best'.

There was a terribly dodgy moment when my mother started talking about her ex-husband, my father, and much to my shock she lifted up her little finger and declared once more that, 'he's only got a penis this big.' 'Muuuum!' I exclaimed with horror, twirling my hair nervously while I felt the blood rushing to my face. I only hope that they were too sozzled with alcohol to notice, or maybe they thought they'd heard wrong because my mother spoke with a very strong Polish accent. Regardless, they were agog at this exotic foreigner and invited us all for dinner the next evening, which I thought was very kind. It seemed that they were bedazzled by my mother and wanted to check her out a bit more.

For the dinner Effie cooked roast lamb, pumpkin and peas and as usual the television was on in the dining room in the background. Garnet and Effie's way of life was so alien to what my mother was used to. They told her that they had never seen a television until they were in their forties and even then they mainly watched *Star Trek*, Garnet's favourite programme. My mother was very polite, obviously feeling kindly condescension for these simple people who probably thought she was some sort of film star.

The next day, Graham and I showed her the sights of Melbourne, such as they were. The weather was very hot, it being February, Australia's hottest month, and my mother started wilting with boredom very quickly. I went to work on the Monday morning as normal, thinking she could perhaps see Effie or wander around the neighbourhood exploring the strange houses and surroundings. When I got home at 6 p.m., to my horror, she was in floods of tears, telling me how bored and lonely she was and how ghastly Melbourne was. I put my arm around her and promised I'd give up work straight away and stay at home with her. I agreed with her that it was awful and cursed Olga for not keeping her mouth shut; if it hadn't been for her, we wouldn't both be in this blinking dump. But we had to make the best of it, there was no choice. She and I walked around the streets the next day amused by the quaint little one-storey houses with concrete drives along each side. They were surrounded by tropical gardens with sweet little letterboxes on sticks at the end of each drive.

My mother wasn't accustomed to the thousands of flies that Australia is famous for but quickly perfected the art of 'the great Australian salute' as we waved our hands in front of our faces nonstop to prevent countless flies sitting on us or crawling on our heads and trying to get into our eyes. Thank heavens she had brought a couple of flimsy frocks but I noticed she was sweating and kept having to wipe her forehead and her black mascara dribbled down her cheeks. Waking up each morning covered in mosquito bites also added to her irritation. Most houses had sprinklers on nonstop outside on their lawns and at every opportunity I'd run through one to cool off but my mother told me I was being very childish. She started picking on me over the slightest thing but I put it down to the heat.

Jane and Tony were the poshest of Graham's friends. Jane had been a nurse and had a fabulous figure, a huge expanse of tanned brown bosom, very bleached hair and appalling teeth, with most missing at both sides. Her husband Tony was a travelling salesman for ladies' knitwear and they had done very well for themselves, managing to buy a pretty old house in East Malvern. They considered themselves very superior, especially as they furnished their house with old furniture and whatever passed for 'antiques', of which they were very proud. All snobs wanted old houses and new builds were very much looked down upon, as is the case to this day. They had been married for five years and had two children and, as they had never been out of Melbourne either, not even to Sydney, they were interested in meeting my mother to see what a Polish person from England looked like and have some diversion from routine humdrum life. Jane had been a previous girlfriend of Graham's and I don't really think she liked me very much. However, I was very grateful to them as I was finding my mother difficult to keep amused. Not much happens in downtown Melbourne and she couldn't cope with the terrible forty-degree heat.

Jane and Tony arranged a BBQ for Sunday afternoon but on the news the day before it was announced that Melbourne had a 'total fire-ban day', meaning that no outdoor fires were allowed because of the risk that the slightest spark could precipitate a bush fire. So we all ate in the kitchen instead, although they didn't have air conditioning. The only way to keep out the heat was to have the venetian blinds half shut and the house was oppressively hot. Jane and Tony also lived in a one-storey house in bland suburbia and we mainly talked about their garden and how fast their eucalyptus trees grew. They were very proud of their lemon-scented gum tree which had white bark and fragrant leaves and my mother politely showed interest in a shrub called Cootamundra wattle, which was bright yellow, but we didn't venture too close to it because it was swarming with bees. Australia seemed to be swarming with all manner of creepy crawlies, stinging critters and wasps the size of flying sausages. We went to the beach but it was too hot. Graham very much enjoyed going to the beach after dark and just sitting on a blanket drinking beer and occasionally swimming but having seen the film *Jaws* I was in no hurry to get into the dark water.

There had been a ten-day hot spell of weather in Melbourne, with no hint of a breeze and we could hardly breathe. My flat was like an oven; the windows caught the afternoon sun and the nights were airless and stifling with only the sound of mosquitoes inside and cicadas outside. My mother slept in my bed whilst I slept on a mattress on the floor; she tossed and groaned with the heat, and every so often would get up and make an alcoholic drink. I could see she couldn't wait to get me married off so she could leave.

As I had no friends or family, it was arranged that Garnet would give me away. As I was shy with Garnet I didn't ask him myself, so Graham did instead. Just before the wedding, Graham and I had been to see the vicar of St Mary's Church in Malvern with my mother, as her signature was required for my marriage because I was under twenty-one. I half hoped she would refuse to sign but she did and I then knew I was doomed. I didn't like the vicar very much either. He was very particular about his services; he wouldn't let me have the music I wanted and also he specifically said that when he asks the question 'who giveth this woman to be married to this man?' Garnet was just to stand wordlessly, passing my hand without saying 'I do'. I thought to myself that this was going to be a disastrous occasion.

I had written to my father that I was getting married and he sent me a magnificent set of copper saucepans, too beautiful to use, I thought. I kept them afterwards displayed on a shelf. I later learnt that my father had suffered from terrible depression after I went to Australia and I was fully aware that it was all my fault. I loved him so much but I must have brought him little joy as a daughter thanks to my mother's unnecessary malice and I felt dreadfully guilty remembering his calm kindness. He never once said any-thing bad about my mother, except that he found it hard to trust her and that I understood as her mood swings were hard to com-prehend. She would be vibrant and jolly one minute and petulant, aggressive and sulky the next.

On the day of my wedding, the weather was stifling and muggy but the weather forecast said a cool change was on the way. My mother helped me into my wedding dress which was slimline and made from white ribbon lace. It was very pretty but I just bought it off the peg with scant enthusiasm. I said I felt I was going to a funeral and it was my shroud and my mother reprimanded me. Before going to the church I posed for photographs in Effie's front garden and countless flies flew around me in the humid weather and got stuck in the netting of my long veil.

I chose for my matron of honour a girl called Margaret McCloony. A hairdresser by profession, she was the only one of Graham's friends who had been remotely nice to me since my arrival and one evening when I had had too much to drink in her company I asked her to be my bridesmaid and she readily agreed. She didn't have many friends and as in psychological studies of schools, the least popular girl always becomes friends with the newcomer. She was rather fat and loud and coarse. The next time I saw her when we were both sober, she gave me the chance to retract my offer because she knew we were pissed but I had given my word and wouldn't hear of it. Graham's snooty friends laughed at my choice because Margaret was dreadfully common and stout with a very thick, boring husband called Ken and they lived in Moonee Ponds which was the most downmarket suburb of Melbourne; an orderly, flat miserable place with miles of identical cream brick-veneer houses, made famous in later years in Dame Edna Everage's monologues. Even my mother asked how I could have chosen her. I couldn't have let Margaret down and withdrawn my offer though because she was so kindly and sweet, though I hardly knew her and in truth after my wedding I never saw her again as Moonie Ponds was miles away and I didn't have a phone or a car.

Being an evening wedding, as is the norm in Australia in order to escape the heat of the day, one of their few customs which I thought sensible and civilised, Garnet and I left for the church at 6 p.m. En route in the car the thunder and lightning started and a sheet of tropical rain lashed down. I wasn't excited at all and Garnet was quiet, withdrawn as usual into his own thoughts, his eyes vacant, although he did say automatically that I looked very nice.

All the guests in the church sat at the front. There were about a hundred of them but before I walked up the aisle it looked very empty from the door. I longed for my London friends, these being all Graham's people and his grumpy, fat ex-girlfriends. The storm raged on outside and a yelping dog ran up the aisle of the church. My mother wore a pale cream ribbon lace frock with a matching jacket and cream hat and Effie wore pale pink silk and her pearls.

Mother Anguish

They were both very friendly to each other on the day and my mother was in a very good mood, as the weather had cooled down and she was leaving Melbourne the next day. By the time the service was over and we posed for photos outside the church, it was already quite dark and the ground very wet from the rain.

There was an evening reception in a local venue; a wooden building not at all grand but suggested by Graham because it was cheap. It all passed in a blur. Telegrams were read out from my friends in England and Graham heckled them snickering and embarrassing me. My wedding night passed in a blur as well as Graham was thankfully drunk. He was unable to consummate the marriage as, upon leaving the reception, his friends had drunkenly and noisily lifted him high up over their heads with unseemly rowdiness to carry him to the car and somehow dropped him on some concrete which left him with back pain.

The next day my mother left by the same ship in which she had come, it having been on a cruise of the South Pacific islands in the meantime. She excitedly told me that awaiting her was an invitation to dine at the captain's table that night and I desperately wanted to go with her. Her ship sailed and she stood waving on the deck. Graham and I threw streamers and the funnels hooted farewell at full blast. It was so emotional as I waved and waved from the dock and the ship pulled away and the last streamer broke. Her first stop was to be Sydney two days later, so Graham and I drove there as part of our honeymoon as I wanted to see my mother one more time. She disembarked but she had little time for me as she had another date with the captain and was very much looking forward to the long voyage. I mournfully took a photo of the ship leaving Sydney harbour on a damp drizzly day. And that was that. I was stuck.

Graham and I flew to Norfolk Island for two weeks. Norfolk is a small volcanic Australian territory in the South Pacific Ocean, 1000 miles south-east of Sydney. It has a fascinating history, having been discovered by Captain Cook in 1774. It is fourteen square miles and served as a penal colony from 1788 to 1825. The very worst offenders were sent there and died there too. I read in a book that the first child ever to be born on Norfolk was to a convict woman and a prison guard and I wondered what had come of that love affair. Norfolk Island is very lush and fertile and in 1856 the inhabitants of Pitcairn Island, which was small and rocky, were moved en masse to begin new lives on Norfolk. The numerous descendants of the mutineers of the *Bounty*, who had been stranded there ever since, and their Tahitian wives needed more room to plant their crops in order to survive and Norfolk was ideal. The island's income now mainly comes from tourism, though having been there I don't think I would recommend it as the waters around are teeming with sharks. The only safe place to swim is Emily Bay, as that has a coral reef, but even then I wouldn't trust it at high tide. Graham and an islander went shark fishing. They would first get a huge bloody chunk of horsemeat and put it on a very large hook, together with a live fish that is still wriggling, before firmly tying the rope on to a solid rock and then sit drinking beer and wait. Terrifying and boring all at the same time just to sit there and wait, with the chance of a great monster with teeth leaping out any minute. The only rubbish dump in Norfolk Island was a cliff called 'Headstone'. Everything got thrown over Headstone and once I saw the islanders chuck a dead horse over and into the sea and the frenzy of instant sharks was enough to give one nightmares for life. The people are odd too, having been inbred for 200 years. I spoke to a local woman who had recently married and she told me her surname was Adams and then said her previous husband was also of the surname Adams, so I asked, 'Goodness, what was your maiden name?' to which she replied 'Adams'. Having been cut off for so long, the islanders have developed their own language which derives from eighteenth-century English and Tahitian. In this patois 'They said' becomes '*Dem tull*' and 'not going' is '*Nor gwen*'. My very favourite, which I heard all the time, is '*No blaa goo*', meaning 'No bloody good'.

Graham moved into my little flat when we returned to Melbourne but I could see that he missed his mother's comforts and the roast lamb dinners. I did my very best with cooking and even made pies with homemade pastry. Back in Melbourne I was so lonely, I didn't have a single friend that I could laugh and gossip with and so against my better judgement I bought a little dog. I wanted to return to England and the laws of quarantine were strict but I desperately needed to lavish my affection on something as I had nothing to love. I returned to work at the bookshop in Myers. Exploring the city I found a pet shop in little Bourke Street which had fluffy Pekingese puppies frolicking on straw in the window and every single day at lunchtime I would grab a sandwich, go there and stand for an hour outside the shop, just gazing at them. They reminded me so much of Trusie, whose loss I still fretted. I bought one of the cream-coloured pups for $30. She had a black face and long black fringing on her ears and tail and I named her Misha and loved her to distraction. She seemed equally devoted to me, obeying every instruction, never leaving my side and sleeping by my bed. We enjoyed going to the beach together at weekends where she dug deep holes in the sand and swam out to sea with me, returning to my husband's surfboard, her long ears flapping in the wind. Later, one of our friends' dogs was taken by a shark and we were told to keep her out of the water as the smell of a wet dog is detected by sharks from a great distance. In our flats dogs weren't allowed but I nevertheless managed to smuggle Misha in without the beady-eyed landlord noticing.

I concentrated on getting pregnant although I told Graham I was on the Pill. Graham and I were not suited for marriage in any way and we were wretchedly unhappy within weeks. He had been an attractive bachelor, much in demand in his circle, and avoided marriage until the age of thirty, hopping from flower to flower and leaving behind a trail of disappointed girls who had succumbed to him too readily. He had a very cruel streak with women and was ruthlessly unkind to any who he had been to bed with and then subsequently dumped. He enjoyed his freedom, travel, surfing and drinking without a care in the world. He even excelled at limbo dancing of which he was very proud, having won a drunken contest. That was his greatest achievement I think. He certainly never read a book or a newspaper and had no interest in anything but women and drink.

My grandmother always told me to never marry out of my own class, otherwise after a while 'his table manners will annoy you' and never was a truer word spoken. Graham used to place as much food as he could into his mouth, forkful after forkful, give it a few chews and then push it to the side of his mouth until it looked as though he had a tennis ball in his cheek. At this point he would start talking and I used to exclaim, exasperated, 'for God's sake swallow it first.' He eventually would, following it with a resounding burp.

Having enjoyed the thrill of the chase where I was concerned, he then resented being a staid married man. I think he equated masculinity with freedom and having been won I was no longer desired, apart from his vengeful need to torment me and prove he was still the mega-stud and Lothario. He was aware that I had no money for my passage home and my vulnerability was his power. He knew I lived desperately for the post from England and he objected vociferously to my excitement whenever I devoured my post and re-read all my letters over and over. He absolutely refused to let me have a phone as it suited him to have me made vulnerable by separation.

He was very highly sexed and I felt he took pleasure in condemning me to a life of sexual servitude and domestic drudgery, complaining constantly that he didn't get enough of his rights as a married man and that I was a lousy housekeeper, which I admit

ABOVE LEFT   Me in London, aged seven, a little scholar with my fountain pen

ABOVE RIGHT   Me, aged about three, with my beloved grandfather Tadeusz

BELOW   Me, aged four, with my magpie

ABOVE   Raba Wyżna in southern Poland. My grandmother inherited the entire estate at the age of twelve

RIGHT   My father, aged about twenty-six

BELOW   Lawday Place, Farnham, Surrey

 VE LEFT   Me, aged ten with my mother, happy on holiday in Italy

VE RIGHT   My mother, aged about twenty-nine, and her lover Mr Kieconski

OW   My mother and Mr Henryk

E LEFT Garnet leading me as a glum bride to my wedding aged eighteen

E RIGHT The lonely house in Melbourne

ɔw The Australian family. From left to right: Ian, his daughter Megan, my daughter Camilla sitting on Effie's knee, Effie with the blue hair, my son Adam, Ian's wife Sandra, and Graham and I at the back. Taken a month before I ran away

ABOVE LEFT   An early modelling picture

ABOVE RIGHT   Me and my children back in London in Hyde Park

ABOVE LEFT   Dick shortly after I met him. Note the scorpion medallion...

ABOVE RIGHT   Post my transformation of him into a gentleman and OBE. Taken at Buckingham Palace in 1994

LEFT   Sam Parker

ABOVE   At Clarence House with Her
Majesty the Queen Mother

RIGHT   At the Queen Mother's Gate
opening ceremony, 6 July 1993

BELOW   The royal stand at the opening
ceremony with me at the far left

Mother Anguish

I was. I hate housework, although I did my best. Once I resorted to shouting at him, saying, 'you don't pay me by the hour!' He would often scream and yell and slam doors because he didn't get enough sex. Once he declared that frustrated men were more likely to die of heart attacks and accused me of depriving him of his needs and thereby shortening his life. He kept calling me a 'stuck-up English prude' and constantly said I was frigid and needed to see a psychiatrist. I was beginning to hate the very sight of him and all his obscure and inconsequential friends but I stayed calm in all situations with a quiet resignation. I won't be here forever, I kept telling myself.

He was also a very heavy smoker and never without a fag in his mouth. He lit up the moment he woke, keeping his cigarettes by the side of his bed and even smoked whilst taking a shower; his ashtray was on the bathroom cabinet and every so often his wet hand would emerge from the shower cubicle and he would take a puff before replacing the fag, the end of which was all soggy. Once I was mystified why my white bathroom ceiling had brown spots all over it and it took me a while to work out that this was caused by nicotine mixing with the steam that rose and settled up high. He even smoked during the sexual act, pausing his thrusting every so often to take a huge puff which would be blown all over my face. Also, as I insisted on having sex in the dark, I was always nervous in case he was careless in the throes of passion and burnt me; as it was, ash dropped on my chest frequently. But as a rule our coupling was quick, with no endearments spoken and then we would sleep as far apart as the bed would allow. I found him uncouth and regretted the day I met him.

Although I was desperately trying to get pregnant, there was a limit to what I could endure and he would set upon me at all hours, especially at weekends when he seemed to have a permanent erection. He would lurch himself on to me constantly and I would make up every excuse I could think of, pretending I was having an extra long period and frequently dissolving into tears. Once, after a particularly lengthy and persistently cruel nagging session, during which he swore brutally, I finally agreed to get it over and done with. I remember sitting in my bed leaning my back against the wall whilst Graham was in the bathroom. The light was on and he entered the room taking long, slow strides, naked except for an inane grin on his face and a huge erection which was bobbing up and down. I felt such a terrible sadness overwhelming me because of what I was about to endure and whimpering pitifully I thought, I want to go home, I want my mother. I didn't have a martyr syndrome; I merely didn't like being impaled by someone not to my liking. I had to get pregnant but there was nothing to boost my libido. I begged the local doctor to give me something so that I could feel some desire or at least endure it, but he laughed. The more I had sex the more I hated it.

The very worst thing about being married was the husband. I am aware that societies are based on marriage and its consequences and do I believe in marriage, it's just the living together afterwards that is the problem. It amused me to think that throughout history a good marriage had been considered a woman's sole vocation in life, preferably with advancement of social status thrown into the bargain. My union with this man was purely for sperm-donation reasons. In the cultured spheres, under which I had been brought up, young ladies were reared to show poise, elegance and refinement to prospective husbands and I was all of that but wasted myself by 'marrying down'; all my upbringing had been for nothing. Marriage across the class divide in history has often worked when a high-achieving man has chosen a bride from the lower ranks. After all, in 1763 the brilliant banker Thomas Coutts had scandalised society by choosing to marry one Elizabeth Starkie, a serving maid in his brother's household. Their marriage lasted fifty years and produced seven children. Learning about this man has always amused me; he must have been a very romantic fellow indeed, as only four days after Elizabeth's funeral he made another controversial marriage, this time to an actress forty years his junior. When he died seven years later, he left his second wife his entire fortune. Other examples of this phenomenon include the fifth Earl of Berkeley, who married Mary Cole, a butcher's daughter, in 1765 and the Earl of Gainsborough, who married his gamekeeper's daughter and lived happily ever after. What fun. But the reverse does not hold true, when a woman trades down and a wife assumes the rank and status of her husband. Graham was a burping boor and I was nothing.

Lying in bed one night in a state of sullen melancholy, I composed a little poem. It went thus:

Is this all that life holds for me, suburbia and drudgery?
Am I to rot here till I die, under this Australian sky?
This cursed place, wherein I cry, bitter tears of my regret.
Of loved ones that I must forget.
Cry scalding tears of homesickness, of wasted youth and loneliness.
And my one life in such a mess.

One Saturday afternoon I was kneeling on the kitchen floor tidying a cupboard and he insisted I oblige him straight away. I used to cry and make excuses but eventually after ceaseless nagging I would anesthetise myself with whisky, swallow two Mogadons and brace myself for his mauling. As I lay on my back, harpooned by this humping and huffing oaf making pig-like noises and while I braced myself against the pain of his manhood, much too large for me to accommodate, I thought of England; of the golden meadows of childhood, the divine town of Farnham in Surrey with its Tudor buildings, the Cotswold stone villages of Gloucestershire, the darling buds of May and the buzz of London. My certainty that one day I would be free was what kept me sane; for I was a prisoner in Australia, much like those poor, wretched convicts of two hundred years ago. Homesickness etches a pain like nothing else.

At last my period was late and I went to the local GP who confirmed my pregnancy. I was dizzy with joy; I was undamaged inside and normal after all. He said that he would care for me during my pregnancy and deliver the baby too. He was very nice and I rejoiced as I walked home on that sunny afternoon. When I told Graham that night he insisted I have a termination as we still lived in a flat. In Australian culture, everyone works towards getting a house first before babies are even thought of.

The very next day he left for work early and we did not speak.

When I went to the bathroom I noticed some blood on my knickers and flew into hysteria at the thought that I was miscarrying. Although I had hitherto kept to myself and stayed away from the neighbours in my block of flats, I dashed to the door across the landing, pounded furiously on it and rang the bell. My neighbour, who I had never spoken to before, opened the door and I told her frantically about the blood and that I was losing my baby. She kindly guided me back to my flat and made me lie down. She had a telephone and as I lay in bed sobbing she rang Effie. My mother-in-law came over and sat on my bed as I told her I was pregnant and bleeding and scared I'd lose the baby but even she said it would be for the best as it's not practical having a baby in a flat. She was appalled by the pregnancy, so gave me no comfort or wise words at all and I didn't know what to expect. How I wished that I had a phone so I could ring my own mother. I had absolutely no one of my own in Melbourne, no family and no thoughtful friends. I lay in bed for days, not daring to move in case the baby fell out and miraculously the bleeding stopped. Perhaps this pregnancy would hold on after all. It was all I cared about and I considered staying in bed for the full nine months if necessary.

I was so anxious that when Sunday came along and Graham wanted to go to Effie and Garnet's for lunch I was afraid to get into

Mother Anguish

the car in case it jiggled. When we arrived, no word was mentioned about my pregnancy and I hugged my joy to myself. Garnet, Effie, Graham and Ian were all silent and refused to speak to me, as they felt I had trapped Graham. Excuse me, I thought to myself, Graham is no great shakes and I thought I was the prize. I sat there sullen and defiant, acting with as much disdain and haughtiness as I could muster, but deep down I was feeling very lost, lonely and frightened. I didn't care if they were interested in the baby or not. It was nothing to do with them; it was purely my baby and they could all get stuffed. The atmosphere was ghastly.

The months followed, I counted the days and measured my expanding waistline with wonder. I had liked the local doctor but after the fright of my bleeding would take no risks and so consulted the most fashionable obstetrician in Melbourne, Professor John Leeton. I had read about him in the newspapers and was determined to have the best. Graham and Effie were astounded that I was brave enough to approach such an eminent and famous man, as he was not for the likes of them, and Graham snidely remarked that 'I had tickets on myself'. I told Professor Leeton all about my abortion and how desperate I was to have this child; how nothing else mattered in my life. He assured me that women often bleed in early pregnancy and I think I developed a huge crush on him. I was so grateful and he was the only person in the whole of Melbourne that was interested in my welfare and showed me genuine kindness. I lived for our monthly meetings and he always seemed pleased to see me. We used to have long consultations which would overrun cheerfully and he was very interested in everything I said. He told me he had an English wife and four children so we would chat happily about England. I adored him; he was forty-two years old, handsome, cultured and what's more he lived in Toorak! How did it happen that I married such a plonker as Graham when there were men like this in the world? He was entirely fabulous and a gentleman of undeniable distinction.

On my first wedding anniversary we were routinely at Effie's house on Thornberry Crescent, eating roast lamb, pumpkin and peas, when Graham said there was a surprise for me in his mother's bedroom where the telephone was. He had booked a three-minute call to my mother as a present; only three minutes, he said, as it was so expensive to call England. I was overjoyed to hear her voice and tried to tell her to prepare for rescuing me as soon as the baby was born, speaking in Polish as Effie and Graham were standing there, but I was totally unprepared for this conversation as phone calls were not the usual; I had got out of the habit as, not having one of my own, I hadn't spoken to anyone at all on the telephone for over a year. In my excitement I talked loudly and desperately but all too soon it was over. I begged for another three minutes and they reprimanded for me for being greedy and never satisfied. 'We are not put on this earth to enjoy ourselves, you know,' said Graham. 'Your life is here now. Put the past behind you and try to settle down.' They told me as usual that England was definitely going to the dogs with power cuts and government problems and I was very lucky to be in Australia. Effie kept telling me that I was selfish for being ungrateful as I had 'everything anyone could wish for' and by that I presume she meant her precious elder son. But I felt that, being well born, educated and cultured, I deserved much better. In fact, that present of his was as good as it got and when I turned twenty-one some time later, no one acknowledged it in any way and I spent my birthday totally ignored at home.

I wasn't sure if these people were stupid or just lacking in education but they didn't know anything. Effie admitted to me that she had sent Graham to the local state school throughout his early life and then, when he was fifteen, sent him to a private school for his final year to 'finish him off'. I pointed out to her that this was entirely the wrong way round and that a sound early education imprints itself on the mind of a child; by the time he was fifteen he would have discovered girls and had no interest in learning at all. Consequently, I discovered too late that Graham as an adult was barely literate; he couldn't spell at all and his handwriting was very childish. Once when he had left a note for me to say he would be coming home late, he spelt it 'laight'. To this day I don't know whether he was dumb, dyslexic or too lazy to try. At his father's firm his job was to drive around visiting clients and touting for business and he was never called upon to sit in an office because of his inability to read and write. In Spain it hadn't occurred to me to test his spelling and grammar. He was just a glamorously hand-some beach bum that all the other girls fancied.

My pregnancy was never mentioned by Graham or Garnet or Effie, not a single word at any time. I was too superstitious to buy a pram or a cot or any baby clothes, I just turned into a solitary cocoon and spent my days laying about and reading. Graham would be out all day and come home late, frequently with a guilty look on his face as I knew he had a fondness for massage parlours. On the evenings when he had visited hookers he would bring me a pizza from the city and a large bottle of gin. When I was six months pregnant Graham came home very late one Friday night. As I had no phone, he couldn't tell me what was keeping him. He entered the flat swaying and drunk and told me his dad Garnet had died of a heart attack in the office at 5 p.m. He had been sitting at his desk and in typical Garnet fashion had slumped down without a word and died. Ian had been sitting close to him but hadn't noticed. Then a distant secretary called out to him asking, 'is your father OK Ian?' He tried to give his dad mouth to mouth resuscitation but it was no good. Graham and I drove straight over to Effie's house and she was sitting calmly in the dining room, having been informed by Garnet's sister Gwen, who was sitting with her holding her hand. 'I am so sorry for you,' I said but she just looked glazed. 'It's funny, I don't feel anything at all,' were her exact words in response. I noticed the bottle of Valium in the kitchen was almost empty.

As he had died on a Friday his wage packet was in his pocket but the undertaker or ambulance man must have nicked it. The next day being a Saturday, the funeral director came to Effie's house to make arrangements and he was very efficient. When told that Garnet had died of a coronary aged fifty-four, he said, 'it happens all the time.' He asked what she would like to do with Garnet's car and she replied that she didn't ever want to see it again, so I don't know what happened to it. Effie didn't want to view the body either and she chose Garnet's coffin from a catalogue. Graham, Ian, Ian's girlfriend Sandra and I all went to Effie's and sat there that day. Ian kept asking about Garnet's will and Graham went rummaging and scavenging through Garnet's clothes. In the funeral cortege the following week, Effie sat in the front car wearing a very jaunty hat with a white feather poking out and Graham and I sat in the second car. Graham was angry at his mother's hat and I giggled. He was a fine one to talk, I thought, as he had helped himself to his father's best suit the very day after he died. It was a dark brown colour and well-tailored and Graham wore it to Garnet's funeral. There was no church for the service, it taking place directly at the crematorium and it was sparsely attended as they had few friends. I was bemused by the absence of any funeral rites. It was so unlike the serious attitude Polish people adopt when confronted by a death; there was no gravity of mourning or the wearing of respectful black, although I was dressed in my black dress and carried a black chiffon scarf. Ian was there with Sandra; their wedding was planned for the following month.

Effie seemed to adjust to widowhood with great ease and never wore anything vaguely resembling subdued attire. The first thing she did was get a hammer and nail pictures into the walls, something which Garnet had never allowed before. I have never known a widow to embrace widowhood with such casual acceptance. Garnet had died as quietly as he had lived and was thereafter unmourned and unlamented. Effie bought herself a number of new clothes, many new twinsets and matching tartan skirts, and also a mouthful of sparkling new dentures and had her hair turned a deeper shade of blue. She had had false teeth ever since her twenties. It was the fashion in Australia of that generation to have your teeth removed; therefore one had no need to see the dentist and saved lots of money. It was also a standard twenty-first birthday present for many girls.

In Garnet's will he left almost all his money to Effie, including the matrimonial home. Fifty-one per cent of the business went to Graham, him being the elder son and forty-nine per cent to Ian who went ballistic and there was much shouting and slamming of doors. Garnet had left by way of compensation only $1000 to Graham and $2000 to Ian. Effie insisted that Graham give up his share and make it fifty-fifty but I protested and stood firm and Graham agreed. Effie and Ian objected to a youngster like me interfering in their family matters but I considered myself capable and astute enough to be able to guide Graham and hoped he might start making some money and stop spending the little bits of cash my mother would include in her letters to me. He insisted that this went on our groceries instead of fripperies and whatever I wanted. No matter how often I said that my mother sent this money to me personally for my own needs, Graham insisted that she meant it for both of us. I had never known anyone so avaricious.

Ian and Sandra got married three weeks later and because of my pregnancy I only had one dress that fitted me. It was a pretty black frock with a white collar and floppy bow. I wore it to Garnet's funeral and also to Ian's wedding and when it was in the wash, I didn't leave the house at all. Graham objected to me buying maternity clothes as it was a waste of money, pregnancy only being temporary. My breasts became so large in my pregnancy that when I was in the city visiting Professor Leeton I bought myself a new, comfortable maternity bra and Graham was furious at my extravagance. I was in need of a new dress but Graham again said, 'we are not put on this world to enjoy ourselves, you know.' I think he felt insecure and therefore aggressive and he always found fault with whatever I was doing and tried to make me feel guilty for foisting this unwelcome pregnancy on him by trickery. He was incandescent with anger that I was pregnant and we never discussed it. Needless to say, I didn't want any sex and refused him throughout as I didn't want anything poking at my womb and disturbing the baby. I can't sew at all but in my desperation I also bought a couple of metres of pink woollen material and set about making my own dress. Stitching it all by hand I even managed to put sleeves into it, though they puckered and when we went to Jane and Tony's anniversary party a lot of people jovially laughed and teased me. Unfortunately when I washed it, it shrunk and I looked ridiculous as it became many inches too short at the front.

Ian's bride Sandra was a pretty girl, with beautiful, thick natural blonde hair and a fine figure but she only had about six teeth. Shortly after her wedding she followed Effie's example and had all her teeth removed aged twenty-two. She then had a full set of dentures and Graham told me later that Ian boasted to him how when she removed her dentures she gave a magnificent blow job. She came from the lowest working-class council estate in Melbourne. She was one of nine children and at the time of her wedding her mother was pregnant again and in her forties. At the reception her parents were very coarse, loud and drunken and I looked upon them with horror. Bloody hell, I thought to myself, as if Graham and his family weren't low enough, now I am allied with the most appalling trash. I think she was sweet-natured though and she tried to befriend me but I didn't like Ian and kept very reserved. I have always felt a bit guilty about my standoffishness, as she died a horrid death aged just thirty-two having contracted lupus, a nasty disease which disfigured her face with a purple rash and also affected her joints so she couldn't move. The doctors overdosed her on steroids and she got the typical moon-like bloated face and neck before her organs totally failed and she developed the serious heart problems of which she died. I felt awful when I heard this as I should have been friendlier to her.

At this time we had a house being built in the bush which took six months. It was Spanish in style and I designed it totally myself, right down to the last power point, trying to make it as beautiful as possible so that when the time came to sell it to fund my escape, we would have a ready market. It was white with an arched entrance, beautifully proportioned rooms, inbuilt bookcases and a spacious kitchen. Graham assured me that that once it was built up the area would become 'the new Toorak' but as usual he was wrong and the house looked dreadfully out of place there years later, where it stands to this day. At the time of its construction it was just on a flat plot of land with no neighbours. Meanwhile we continued to live at the flat.

One day when I was returning from the local milk bar, a straggly, skinny dog, about six months old, limped up to me, his hind leg all bloody. He had obviously been in an accident and I took pity on him, letting him follow me home where I gave him a blanket and some food. He licked his wounds and within a fortnight not only was he was healed but twice his original size and gloriously bright and affectionate. I called him Fluff because he had none. It was arranged that my mother-in-law would care for Misha while I was in the hospital giving birth but she refused to take Fluff as well. My brother-in-law Ian had sneered at me disapprovingly for having bought a pedigree dog like Misha when there were so many unwanted and unloved strays in the world and he always spoke of wanting a dog himself, so I thought Fluff would be just perfect for him. I offered it to him but he had some feeble excuse. By now the landlord had noticed my two dogs and threatened to evict us and everyone pressured me to give Fluff to the police station, who would find him a good home. My husband said I would have enough work when the baby came and, what with having Misha, I couldn't keep a large dog as well. He drove me to the police and I cried as I pulled at Fluff's lead while he stared up at me bewilderedly. I never saw him again. I am sure he was put down as Melbourne had a huge stray dog problem. A short while later Ian proudly bought himself an expensive Doberman and Rottweiler crossbreed and I was so struck by his unfeeling hypocrisy that I never spoke to him again. As for Sandra, in my eyes she was guilty by association, so I didn't speak to her either.

Our weekly dinners at Effie's became awkward, unpleasant occasions. Nobody got a civil word out of me. They hated me because I was pregnant and I hated them because of their lack of interest in my baby and general health, so I used to sit there sullen with my arms folded. In truth I was surprised they didn't set up a collection to get rid of me and pay my fare back to London but anyway I would have been too afraid to go on a long flight and risk miscarrying. I hoped against hope that my mother might fly out for the birth as I desperately needed someone to support me but she did not as she was too afraid of leaving Stefan in case he gambled. When she came out for my wedding he managed to gamble away £24,000 in a single night.

Professor Leeton, who by now I was joyfully seeing once a week, decided to induce the baby a month early due to my high blood pressure, so my birth was all pre-planned with no mad dash to the hospital. One Monday afternoon I took my little suitcase, caught the tram to the city and admitted myself to the maternity ward. Graham was at work and showed no interest at all in my impending labour. It was decided he would go to Effie's for dinner and would be informed when the baby was born. I was washed, shaved, prepped with a colonic enema (so undignified) and then my waters were surgically broken by Professor Leeton, who smiled and said, 'see you soon.'

Labour started a few hours later and went on for ten hours with no anaesthetic apart from gas and air, which seemed worse than useless. I was left howling in the room by myself and every so often a midwife came in and told me to stop making so much noise, after which they listened to the foetal heartbeat and went away. At about midnight they must have decided the time had come and they called Professor Leeton, who I was overjoyed to see as he powerfully marched into the delivery room. The midwives' attitude changed instantly and they treated him with obsequious, grovelling respect. I watched him lovingly as he scrubbed up for about ten minutes right up to his elbows. Then he hoisted my legs into stirrups, sat on a stool between my legs at the end of the delivery table and waited between contractions with his hand on his chin. When it got bad forceps were used and he pulled hard at the baby's head. Finally he asked if I might like to see the baby's head protruding out of me. The two midwives helped me to sit up and I was awestruck with wonder at this tiny, shrivelled head with a big nose poking out between my legs. Then I collapsed and with the next contraction the rest slipped out and I was informed I had a son.

They weighed him and promptly took him away to the premature babies ward. I experienced none of this modern skin-to-skin contact where the baby is placed him on the mother's tummy; they just wrapped him up, showed him to me briefly and removed him without me even having a hold. One often hears of babies being muddled up in the hospital nursery but I knew I would recognise him later as he had such a huge nose. They then wrapped me up in hot blankets which felt wonderful and I remained in the delivery room for a little while, exhausted and exhilarated. I was conscious of Professor Leeton tidying up and rattling about a bit and when he came close to me I grabbed his coat with all my strength and tugged saying 'thank you' and he said I had been a good brave girl. I was then trolleyed to my room to sleep. The next day they brought me the baby to see but I wasn't allowed to feed him as they said he weighed under five pounds was therefore too small and would only get exhausted. The nurses would feed him with a tube and I was very upset as I wanted to breastfeed him myself. He became very jaundiced and orange but I was told that that was usual in premature babies.

Graham and Effie came in the morning but didn't bring a present. They viewed the baby through a glass window and didn't say much on their brief visit except that bottle feeding was far more hygienic and breastfeeding was disgusting and only for common people. I named him Adam Garnet out of respect but goodness knows why; I must have been deranged, as I didn't even like Garnet and Effie didn't comment or thank me. I had considered calling him Joe after my father, but I knew my mother would have a fit as she hated my dad and I didn't want to upset her.

I stayed in hospital for a week and was deliriously happy. Because I was so young and had no mother to help me, Professor Leeton arranged for me to go to an aftercare hospital together with the baby, where I would be taught how to look after him. This institution was housed in a huge, forbidding-looking Victorian mansion in large grounds and was a training college for the Australian equivalent of Norland nannies. It was also where babies that were to be given up for adoption were deposited for six weeks while the birth mother was given time to decide if she wanted to give up her baby or not. The girls that were training to be professional nannies were taught their craft by caring for these babies, this being overseen by much older teacher nannies. The academy also had ten private rooms where they took in girls like myself, who knew nothing and had no advisors or mother and I was taught along with the nannies how to care for my child. It was a very interesting time. I had a room of my own but could go to the nursery whenever I wanted and they did all they could to help me develop the mothering skills I needed. As it turned out I had a wonderful two weeks living there, learning a lot and Professor Leeton visited me a few times in the evening on his way home.

Mother Anguish

My baby grew a big tooth in his bottom jaw and when people heard of it, everyone seemed to want to stick their finger into his mouth and feel it. I grew wild with irritation as it was so unhygienic since no one thought of washing their hands beforehand. After a while the tooth started wobbling and I was worried that he might choke on it whilst feeding from his bottle but Professor Leeton had a dentist friend who came over and pulled it out. I recently Googled Professor Leeton and although he is old and grey now, his eyes are as kind and twinkly as ever and I read that he was one the chief pioneers of IVF in Australia and, indeed, the world.

One evening Graham visited me with his ex-girlfriend Jane and they left together. Good luck to them I thought. As soon as I was able, I left Adam in the communal nursery and caught the tram to the British embassy in the city. I put Adam's name on my passport, planning to escape as soon as possible. I wrote to my mother to say we were alive and well and asked her to please send a bit more money for my fare but she refused, saying a screaming baby in the house would disrupt Stefan. Also she didn't want anyone knowing she was a grandmother, as she was then only around forty years old and far too pretty. The first night I brought the baby home to the flat, I was so tired and disappointed that I told Graham I didn't love him at all and that I was going home no matter what. His face darkened with rage and he shouted at me, 'you are not taking that baby out of this country!'

My early days of motherhood were difficult; I had never even seen a naked baby before my own and was totally unprepared. I bought a book called *Dr Spock's Baby and Childcare* and that became my bible but I missed the constant support of the nurses at the aftercare home. My nervousness must have transmitted itself to the baby, who cried a lot in the night even when I had his cot by the side of my bed so I could rock him. When I was at the chemists, some kind assistant recommended a dummy for the baby, which I bought and it worked a treat. Effie was disgusted and told me, 'only common babies have dummies.' She showed little interest in the baby and I never asked her to babysit as I was so thrilled and besotted by my little son that I didn't leave him alone for a minute and I didn't want anyone else to touch him or hold him. Effie kept telling me that I would spoil the baby by hugging him and that I should put him down and let him cry so that he learnt early who was in charge. She told me that when she had Graham she used to put his pram far away at the bottom of the garden and he would scream for hours. She didn't approve of 'feeding on demand' and insisted I only fed the baby once every four hours. She kept instructing me on the right way to do things, all of which went against my instincts. I was in disbelief at her methods and thought, no wonder you've got two thick, screwed-up sons. I indignantly ignored everything she said and with an insolent look on my face told her, 'It's my baby and I'll hold him and hug him as much as I please.' In exasperation I told Effie that she was violating my human rights under the terms of the Magna Carta and I think at that moment she thought that I was mad but it pleased me to see her bottom lip quivering. Graham and Effie insisted that he be circumcised but I point-blank refused as I had seen other babies in the communal nursery with their little willies wrapped up in bloodied gauze and I couldn't bear the thought of inflicting any pain on mine. After a while Effie stopped coming over.

Life assumed a circle of monotony revolving around feeding times and trying to get some sleep. Though certainly weary and stressed, I didn't have post-natal depression as I was thrilled with my child and even when he was asleep I couldn't take my eyes off him, marvelling at every little development and change. At a month old he was already smiling at me and I rejoiced. I rocked him and sang to him, glorying in my extraordinary achievement of motherhood and blessing my luck each day.

Further letters to my mother followed, we wrote two or three times a week, and I was gobsmacked when she suddenly announced that as Stefan was too much of a drunken embarrassment in London, they had both decided to come to Melbourne and enjoy the sunshine. I was absolutely horrified but she assured me that Stefan would be dead very soon and then she and I would both return home. The lease was up on Elvaston Place and I wrote back, 'For God's sake don't sell the great house in Bolton Gardens' but my mother said it was full of sitting tenants which were a nuisance and what's more, the house was overrun with drug addicts who refused to pay the rent. 'It doesn't matter,' I pleaded, 'we can gradually do a deal and winkle out the ones on the first floor and live there, or we can chuck out the housekeeper and live in the basement.' It was such a beautiful house, of six storeys, and in a lovely street and I kept writing to her in desperation, begging her not come here. Melbourne was deadly dull, as she well knew from her visit two years before. But her mind was made up.

Last week I was in the area and walked past the house, which is in perfect condition, freshly painted window frames complementing the brown brickwork, and was told by an expert that it is now worth at least eleven million pounds.

Chapter 7

I wrote to my mother's best friend Krystina and told her I was very unhappy in Australia and asked her to talk my mother out of emigration as I was out of my wits with worry and desperate to come home to London. Krystina replied by return post that my mother had fallen in love with the ship's captain that she had met on her previous voyage and when not at sea he was resident in Sydney. Therefore, my mother's determination to come to Australia was to be closer to him and nothing to do with wanting to see me.

I resolved in desperation to go the city and ring my mother on a public phone and try and talk some sense into her. I lied to Graham and said I needed to go to the dentist and asked him please could he give me a lift to the city when he went to work in the morning. I appealed to Effie to come and babysit, which she was happy to do as she thought me an overanxious mother because I never left him with anyone, taking him wherever I went. However, after accepting the arrangement, she grasped her chance to lecture me on the benefits of dentures: 'I had all my teeth out at twenty years of age,' she said, 'and I haven't had a speck of trouble since. Dentists are a dreadful waste of money and you should have yours removed, just like Sandra did.' Whenever she lectured me on this count, I always replied that I had good, strong white teeth and intended to keep them. By this point there existed a cool, aloof politeness between us and though I used to give her the occasional superior glance of incredulous resentment and mockery, while purposefully gazing at her increasingly blue hair, I was never downright rude and never raised my voice; I perfected an insolent look which the poor woman could not fathom or respond to. She once called me 'rebellious' and I shrugged with indifference. Surely I won't be bothered with these people for much longer, I thought. Furthermore, she was always much against me going to the city as I used to buy a copy of the *Daily Mail* and a few English magazines which she considered a bad influence on me. 'You have to put all thought of England behind you,' she would say, 'you have to settle down; your life is here now and England is going to the dogs.' She used to repeat those last words at every opportunity, like a mantra. Graham once came home and said: 'I have been talking to Mum and she says you are to stop buying English newspapers as it unsettles you.' I always replied to this that it was of no consequence to me whatsoever what his mother thought and that I had no intention of condescending to any discussion about it. 'I shall do as I please; it's not negotiable and not debatable.' Then Graham would sulk and that suited me fine as I could finish my housework and read a book. Books were my only escape.

There was a ten-hour time difference between Australia and England and so I was sure to reach my mother in the evening there. I had no money apart from my pitiful 'running away fund' but that had dwindled as I had needed to buy a pram and baby clothes. When I worked in the book department at Myers I had met a woman called Vicky there who owned a little shop. I knew she admired a beautiful cashmere outfit of mine, a finely knitted pale grey top and skirt with a band of yellow at the neck and at the hem. I had bought it years before at a shop called Continental Boutique opposite Harrods and it was the last of my really expensive items of clothing, the one which I had kept for very special occasions. So we did a deal and in lieu of money she got the outfit while I could use her phone. Phone calls to England were a real expense in those days. Whilst I was trying to get through to my mother via the operator, I was so hurt to see Vicky wasting no time and already happily sitting with a pair of scissors, unpicking the lining of my skirt to alter it to fit her. I felt she should have at least waited until after I had gone.

I remember how wonderful it was to hear my mother's voice when I was put through but she seemed not to grasp the severity of what I was saying and she didn't sound altogether sober either. She kept asking if I was happy there and I kept answering, 'No, it's terrible here, you will loath it. I can't stand Graham, I hate the weather, the flies, the isolation.' I told her how awful the home-sickness would be for her: 'Melbourne is not exactly a repository of culture and you will miss the London theatres and your friends. I would do anything for the sight of a London bus, to hear the rattle of a taxi and to see a wet pavement with the city's glinting streetlights reflected on it.' I tried so hard to remind her that the last time she was in Melbourne, she had wept as it was so awful. 'There is no pain like homesickness, it gnaws away at your soul and one can think of nothing else.' I begged her not to come and again implored her not sell the house at Bolton Gardens but she main-tained her desire to get away to the sun and told me that Stefan was so ill he was unlikely to survive the journey to Australia. She said the doctors had reliably informed her he would live no longer than a year, possibly six months, as he had a brain tumour, recently diagnosed, and there was no hope for him at all. She promised me, just as she had done in all her letters when the word 'promise' was underlined, that as soon as he died, we would return to London.

She told me that she had been hard at work dismantling our home at Elvaston Place, which conjured up a mournfully nostalgic picture in my mind of all that lovely furniture and the wonderful view from my window along Queen's Gate Place, the area that I loved. She had put most of the furniture up for sale at auction and the paintings had gone to Sotheby's. Other knick-knacks she had sold off foolishly cheap to sundry friends who would come around enthusiastically, like vultures, and depart with suitcases full of sil-verware and treasures. Bloody hell, I thought, and I was overcome with horror at imagining this spectacle. But I realised that since Elvaston Place was a three-storey residence and as every room and wall was crammed, there would have been a lot to be got rid of. It was so sad to think of the removal vans and visualise the workmen up on ladders taking down the pictures. Although it was Stefan's home, I nevertheless appreciated its beauty. I had grown to love its proportions and remembered my room with all of Mr Kieconski's cream and gilded furniture.

When my mother told me that Stefan spent all his time ill in bed, unable to cope with the destruction of his home and that she had to oversee the entire dismantling, I was terrified, positive that she would be taken advantage of as she was so silly. 'What about the Jaguar car?' I asked. She told me that a man had come round and told her it wasn't worth much but that 'he was willing to take it off her hands'. She told me he had given her £300 for it. Stefan also had a dinky, little black-and-white convertible Morgan car, which he rarely used as he was mostly too drunk to drive, and she had got rid of this also. My mother had never learnt to drive and did not set much store by cars. In the end I reluctantly acquiesced to her visit. In truth, she didn't sound sober at all and the conversation left me desolate. I was disconsolate and much troubled. But even so, she was my mother and just maybe she was right, maybe we would go back and buy another house. After all, I loved her so much that I could stick it out in Australia for a bit longer to make her happy and also I would have the joy of seeing her every day. I was still young so a few extra months wouldn't kill me. She had said they might buy a little block of flats in Melbourne and live off the rental income and I was so lacking in maternal help and emotional connection that I convinced myself it might work out once she was here. Everything she said made me uneasy but I was longing to see her all the same and I had no alternative but to make preparations for her arrival.

When the baby was six weeks old and I was dizzy with exhaustion, we went one Saturday afternoon for a BBQ at a friend's house. I should have left Misha at home as I had to carry the baby in a carry-cot but I loved my little dog and took her everywhere. A girl called Lynn asked if she could walk her across the road as she was going to buy some cigarettes but I firmly said no, as Misha was a one-woman dog and she didn't know Lynn. I was reprimanded impatiently by Lynn's husband and mocked by the others while Graham swore at me for being so fussy and said I was a 'bloody stuck-up pommy bitch'. Graham was always swearing at me for being deliberately unfriendly to his Aussie mates so I gave in reluctantly. Lynn and Misha went off while I watched from the front garden. Misha somehow slipped her collar off while pulling her head backwards, wanting to run back across the road to me. As I realised the danger from the traffic, I dumped the baby and ran forward shouting, 'Stay, stay!' She was always such an obedient dog but this time she rushed towards me and was run over by a Volkswagen while my legs gave way with shock and I crumpled to the ground, pounding my fists on the pavement and howling with agony. Lynn's husband grabbed me by the arms and tried to force me back into the house and I fought him off. Everyone else was quiet and comforted stupid Lynn instead, who screamed and screamed like a mad woman. We gathered up what was left of beloved Misha and buried her in Effie's garden and I was so numb and dreadfully grief-stricken that I have almost no recollection of the following days. I vaguely remember returning home and walking slowly up the stairs to our flat with Graham and Adam and the heartbreak of tidying up and throwing away Misha's bedding and her toys. Only that morning I had had a dog that loved me and lived for me and now she was gone for ever. Such a short, little life. Even Graham wept. I felt like saying, 'it was all your fault,' but took pity on the man, as he already knew that.

Meanwhile, the house in Templestowe was being built and I was hurrying the builders to finish in time for my mother's arrival. Initially this project all came about while Graham and I were taking a recreational Sunday afternoon drive. There was nothing whatsoever to do on Sundays in Melbourne, so 'going for a drive' was the standard way to spend the day. Far out of town, we came across a new road and a man sitting in a car. He leapt out and did a very hard sell on us, trying to convince Graham to buy a plot of land there as it would be a wonderful investment and land in the area would go up in price. Impulsively we signed up and it was arranged that we would pay it off in instalments. I felt it would do no harm and I could make a tidy profit selling it on the following year.

Templestowe was a very hilly area and our plot of land was on a high point with clear views to the Dandenong hills. It was a lovely house and I enjoyed playing at being an architect, despite never having any tutoring in the subject. I imagined all the finest features I had ever seen in the houses I admired in my childhood and incorporated them into this one. It had sash windows in every room, which was unusual in modern houses and Graham thought it old-fashioned but I insisted. The front door was approached by a balustraded staircase and I made it as grandly imposing as I could. Beyond that I had a ten-foot square hall that I considered gracious but that Effie and Graham said was a ridiculous waste of space. Leading from there to the right-hand side I had three reception rooms in a row, one leading into another with elegant glass-fronted doors. These included a sitting room with a large mantelpiece housing an open fireplace with a chimney. Effie and Graham were also speechless that I insisted on this, as modern, efficient homes were supposed to have ducted central heating. Effie had had gas or electric heaters in her house and she never met anyone who had an open fireplace for burning wood as that was reportedly what common people did. Unfortunately we could not afford central heating but I thought that soon we might have a bit more money and then get it installed. The house had the most beautiful kitchen with a cooking range set into a white arched painted-brick inglenook, such as I had once seen in a magazine. It also had a whole wall of windows looking out on what would eventually be a lush garden. At the moment it was just a muddy building site but I had great plans for eventually transforming it and planting decorative trees such as jacaranda and bougainvillea alongside an elegant lawn. And I would also plant lots of rhododendrons, just like we had in Lawday Place. When the time came for us to sell it, I envisioned a queue of eager buyers and complimented myself on my enterprise at being a property developer aged just twenty-one. Graham accepted all my designs and ideas and was occasionally even keen on my taste, although it was all too baffling for the poor old builder. We drove over there almost every day to hurry along the builders so that it would be ready for Mum and Stefan, as there was certainly no room for them in our flat. Funnily enough, they did finish the very day before but the lavatory wasn't yet attached to the sewage system and there was only a primitive builders' Portaloo in the backyard for the time being. The house was in the prettily named Sassafras Drive but the reality was bleak outer-suburban bush with no neighbours, no transport to the city and surroundings of mud. Graham and I moved in at night-time, grabbed some sleep and leapt out of bed in the morning to get to the airport and welcome my mother.

When I met Mother and Stefan coming out of the gate, I wept as I hugged her with the sheer relief of at last seeing her again. She had put on a bit of weight but was still only around forty-one and pretty. Stefan was dressed in a pale cream suit but he was puffy faced and staggering. I had not seen him since I was eighteen but greeted him courteously. How strange that now he would be living in my house, on my territory and I wondered how things would pan out.

We went straight to our new house, which had no curtains and therefore no covering for the windows as I certainly wasn't going to resort to venetian blinds. It was furnished with old furniture which I had rescued from junk shops and reconditioned. I showed her and Stefan to their room. My mother and I chatted and unpacked whilst Stefan sat in the kitchen with Graham and asked for whisky. By the end of the day both of them were blotto and I felt it boded badly for the future. My mother, I noticed, also drank huge amounts but I wanted them to feel at home so I organised a welcome party for the following Saturday and invited all our friends and also a nice older Polish couple who I had met by chance in the bookshop when he was buying a book about Krakow, where he had been born; of course we had gotten into conversation and I told him that my family originated from Krakow also, although I had never been there.

It was marvellous to meet a Polish man. His name was Guido Lorraine and he had been a well-known actor, quite a star in fact, having appeared in British films such as *The Colditz Story* and *Blue Murder at St Trinian's*. He was very handsome and always got parts in English films whenever they had a casting for a foreign smoothie. He could also sing and dance and told me that his first job in England was singing whilst playing the accordion and skating on ice all at the same time. I liked him and his wife very much; he was great fun and he was also stuck in Melbourne, homesick for England, having gone to Melbourne to do an onstage musical called *Grab Me a Gondola* and somehow got stuck. Guido and his wife couldn't stand Graham, their distaste for him originating from the time that they unexpectedly paid me a visit just before I was due to go into hospital to give birth. They couldn't ring me to say they were coming as I had no phone, so they just turned up with a present of a Moses basket and a little baby's blanket. It was a Saturday afternoon and Graham had been drinking heavily. He welcomed the Lorraines, offering them a chair, and then, as he went to sit down himself, he totally missed his seat and crashed backwards to the floor and on to his backside. I was so embarrassed to see him so drunk and undignified and Mr and Mrs Lorraine were disgusted by the sorry sight of Graham just lying there supine, giggling to himself, half undressed and with his beer gut bulging. I suffered all the humiliations of being a drunkard's wife. Mrs Lorraine looked at me compassionately as they were leaving and said, 'You poor, poor thing.' I was too embarrassed to say anything in return. I recently Googled Guido Lorraine and saw that he died many years later aged ninety-seven, having fallen over and bumped his head on New Year's Eve. Typical Guido. That's the way to go; happy and cheerful and he wouldn't have known what hit him.

I tried so hard to make my mother's party a success but by evening time, when my guests arrived, Stefan was drunkenly slumped in a chair and noncommittal, which was very embarrassing. I was aware my friends were not at all impressed and thought my stepfather not worthy of respect but I put a brave face on and explained to them that he had a brain tumour and was very ill.

Guido and his wife, both teetotallers, promised me that the following week they would take my mother and Stefan out for the day to have a picnic and show them the botanical gardens and other delights Melbourne had to offer. A few days later, the Lorraines came by car to pick up Mum and Stefan for the arranged outing and I was aghast that my mother had filled a Lucozade bottle with diluted whisky. She said that this would keep them going throughout the day and as it was the same colour as Lucozade, the Lorraines would not notice. Of course they did and no further invitations were forthcoming.

Things went from bad to worse. Stefan continually sat in the kitchen, smoking morosely and obviously bored. He complained that he'd never seen so much glass in a house in all his life and I reassured him that I intended to buy some curtains as soon as possible. He was too frightened to go for walks as he had tried it once and in the long grass further away he had seen a large snake. Also, he had come across a deadly redback spider which Graham swiftly killed, being used to these things. 'But this is Australia,' I said, in response to his grumbling, 'you knew it was full of spiders and snakes and nasty things in the water. Be grateful that we are not further north where black widow spiders are found whose single bite kills you stone dead.' One never finds any of these horrors in Knightsbridge. Oh, how I yearned for Knightsbridge. I was unbearably unhappy.

My mother took over the cooking and helped herself to the three beautiful copper saucepans which my father had sent me. I told her I would prefer to keep them on the shelf as decoration only but she told me not to be so childish. A couple of times my mother said to me that when she was my age, her figure was much better than mine and her waistline far smaller. I was hurt and thought it an unnecessarily unkind comment but didn't say anything as I thought my figure was fine. As the weather was so hot she wore her bikini around the house. It was the norm in the heat; lots of people did it and so did I. I noticed that often Graham would put his arm around her waist and say, 'what a lovely mother-in-law I have got,' but for the most part I didn't think much of it and I was very pleased they got on so well. Occasionally though, I thought he was overly tactile and I was uneasy at his creepiness. One time we went to Jane and Tony's to spend the afternoon by their swimming pool and Stefan stayed at home. Anyone possessing a swimming pool was assured plenty of friends. Everyone had drunk a lot of wine and were jumping in and out of the water when suddenly, to my horror, I saw Graham leap on my mother and start tearing off her swimming costume. I'll never forget seeing her semi-doubled over, half-heartedly preserving her modesty as he was pulling down her bikini bottoms. He was laughing and she was laughing also as he stripped her stark naked in front of me and two other people. It was a great joke for them but I was humiliated beyond belief. 'For God's sake, behave yourself!' I exclaimed, glowering with disapproval and sheepishly she put her swimsuit on again. We left shortly afterwards and I wasn't happy wondering whatever had happened to my mother's brain to behave in such an unruly way. It was so undignified.

After Mother and Stefan had been in Melbourne a fortnight, the crate of their remaining furniture from Elvaston Place arrived by ship. Although it had been sent by a professional carrier and everything was wrapped in straw-like stuffing, two chandeliers were smashed and a few things damaged. It took a couple of days to unpack and I felt so sentimental to see some of the beautiful furniture of my childhood. I was astounded, however, at the depressing smallness of the crate. Graham and Stefan unpacked it outside while I watched with sadness. We piled all their belongings into Mum and Stefan's room and she referred to it as a 'mini Elvaston Place'. I asked whatever had happened to my beautiful dressing table that Mr Kieconski had made with the matching mirror and footstool and my lovely desk with a fold-down lid and she told me she had given all his stuff away to friends in London who were only too happy to take it. I bet they were. How could she give away my beautiful dressing table? It was so elegant. But she brought the mirror and the footstool. I think seeing all their antique belongings from London sitting incongruously in a new-build Australian house tipped them over the edge. Stefan got terribly drunk and aggressive. 'Whatever is the matter?' I asked my mother and she angrily told me that Stefan had been so looking forward to coming to Australia and was now very disappointed by it and wished they hadn't come. 'But I told you not to come,' I said with horror. 'I begged you not to come!' Stefan went to his room, nailed blankets on to the windows, shut the door and took to his bed, refusing to come out. Without air conditioning the house was stifling and he cocooned himself in a hot, sticky room.

My house was too isolated without neighbours, there were too many mosquitoes and spiders, the shops were too far away to walk to and they hated it here. I sometimes observed my mother's eyes glittering with something akin to hatred and all my hopes for the future evaporated. I had to accept that they both had a serious drinking problem and I was plunged into misery and felt condemned, as obviously my mother was not going to provide me with any help, comfort or hope of salvation and rescue. My idealised image of her was shattered. Whilst I knew she sometimes had the brain of a child, and not a very bright one at that, she was nevertheless capable enough with her capacity for plotting and scheming and right then she had let me down terribly by solely thinking of herself. Something made me think that things did not work out with her ship's captain; I did ask her about him and she readily admitted to her infatuation but would give no further details except that Stefan would soon be dead and her life would be better. In my naivety I had expected my mother and Stefan to be two dependable adults that would support me emotionally in my life in Australia and instead I had these two dreadful burdens.

Elvaston Place was no more, the pretty farm in Devon had been sold and my mother had sold the fabulous house in Bolton Gardens after all. I had nowhere to go in London even if I did return. My father had remarried a woman with two children so there would be no place for me there. Life was so boring; my mother and I went on walks every afternoon pushing the pram and in the evening she drank herself into a stupor. She neglected her appearance and seldom put on make-up. For that matter, I neglected mine too; I just tied my hair back in an elastic band every day and got on with life tending the baby which was my only joy. I developed an interest in photography and photographed the baby non-stop. Graham complained bitterly at the expense of developing the prints and insisted I limit myself to only one Kodak film a week of only twelve exposures. I often asked him to photograph me holding the baby but he would never agree to more than two shots at a time

Graham's penny pinching was astonishing. He was forever telling me not to flush the lavatory too often as the water rates were expensive and if I had to, then to 'just give it a little flush'. He objected to me buying Macleans toothpaste as there were far cheaper brands available. Graham tormented and berated me at every opportunity and whenever I had a daily bath he would say I was 'wallowing in my own filth' as he preferred showers. Graham decided it was impractical for me to have shoulder-length hair now that I was a married woman and insisted I cut it short to save time which I could utilise better doing my housework. Everything I did was wrong and days of disagreeable structure and tedious routine followed. I was overwhelmed with housework, having no dishwasher or washing machine and I felt my life was being eroded. He considered it a shameful squandering of money to use to more than two sheets of lavatory paper; he would actually eavesdrop outside the bathroom door to hear how much the loo paper holder rattled when used. I listened to him with incredulous distaste but he told me I should be grateful to him as he had given in to my demands for getting a telephone.

My mother was overly attentive to Adam and on one occasion she said to me, 'How funny, a few weeks ago the baby had never met me and now he prefers me over you.' I was hurt by her insensitivity but didn't say anything back. A couple of days later, however, when the baby had toppled over and hurt himself and she had swooped in ahead of me to pick him up and joggle him, I grabbed the baby from her in a moment of frustration, saying, 'It's my child.'

I picked and scratched at my mosquito bites and made a mess of my face with scabs but I was almost past caring, having found myself in such a mess. We had no social life and never went anywhere apart from Effie's once a week so it didn't matter what I looked like. I was so fearful for the future and dazed with despair, seeing no hope at all. Bloody hell, I am going to die out here, I thought. I am going to grow old and ugly with overwork and unhappiness and become an ordinary Australian housewife and eventually turn to drink and gulp Valium like everyone else and die. I didn't want my bones to lie there for ever.

Stefan and my mother lived with us for two months getting drunk with Graham every night and then bought themselves a small house nearby. It was three bedroomed and very ugly and modern, a typical Melbourne bungalow with a flat roof, a carport and a large garden. It was not in their taste or in mine but it was the closest property we could find and the previous owner was very keen to sell quickly as his wife had just died of cancer and he wanted to return to Queensland with his small daughter as soon as possible. He had even had his cat put down, he told me. How awful, I thought, surely he should have asked whoever was buying the house whether they wished to inherit a cat also. Knowing how territorial cats are, I realised that it might be a nuisance taking it to Queensland but even so his behaviour was a bit extreme. Mum and Stefan moved their London furniture out and arranged it as artistically as they could in that incongruous house and then adjusted to their new life. Their only pleasure apart from the drink was their garden and Stefan spent each day in it unshaven and still wearing his dressing gown. He showed no signs of dying but drank great quantities of whisky and flagons of sherry. These would be delivered regularly as Stefan was unable to go to the shops.

The Lorraines had given me their old television, so at least I had a window into the world and Graham busied himself creating a garden and building a fence. Graham was too stingy to buy a new double bed for us so we kept the old one that was given to us by Ken and Margaret before we got married, which they had used for ten years of their married life. Before that it had been given to them by Ken's elderly parents when they bought a new one. In fact, Ken told us that his father had died in it so that mattress must have been a good thirty years old. I shudder to think of all the germs, sperms and insect life it must have contained. It was lumpy and sagged in the middle from age but Graham put a wooden plank beneath it in the middle so at least we didn't roll into each other. The state of the mattress, however, did nothing to interfere with Graham's overwhelming sexual needs. Many was the time when I was fast asleep and I would wake to find him on top of me, either gripping me by the throat or putting his hand over my mouth to stop my objecting as he swiftly entered me before I hardly knew what was happening. It was all over in a matter of minutes and he would roll over to his side and resume snoring. I developed such a hatred and distaste for the sexual act that always the next day I would go about my housework kicking the furniture, saying to myself 'I'm never going to do it again, I'm never going to do it again,' and when I went out with the pram I would kick stones along the way saying the same.

I found it impossible to accept the man's advances as I didn't like him and sex was the main thing that Graham and I fought about. I not only didn't like him, I was starting to loathe him. But my disinterest in him only increased his desire. He made matters worse by swearing and insulting me, constantly calling me a 'horrible, little English prude' because I refused to have sex with the lights on; I just couldn't bear to see him on top of me. If it had to happen, I always wanted it to be done with the utmost speed and the least visibility possible so then I could try to forget about it. For the sake of peace I submitted a few times whilst my mother and Stefan were living in the house as I did not want them to hear us fighting. But once they lived elsewhere, the atmosphere between Graham and me was tense and explosive as he watched me with a lustful eye, especially at weekends. I kept my knickers on in bed for protection, but he would push them aside. I tried to make myself as unattractive as possible and never wore make-up but it was no good; there he always was with that look of leering lust and angry entitlement. Despite his constant advances, he gloried in trampling down my self-esteem and kept telling me how ugly I was becoming, often saying, 'Why can't you be more like your mother?'

The atmosphere out there in the suburbs was very sexually charged; nobody seemed to be happily married to anyone and everyone wanted a bit of sex elsewhere. Whenever Graham and I went to dinner parties at people's houses, most of our friends would want to end the evening with a game of 'strip poker', which, to Graham's supreme irritation, I always emphatically declined to participate in. Graham had heard that there was a wife-swapping group nearby and this excited him into a frenzy, so he nagged and nagged me to come along and join in. I furiously and contemptuously refused, declaring that, 'I am not a suitcase, nobody takes me anywhere and swaps me!' It was ghastly to imagine the fat, drunken nutters throwing their keys into a basket and the poor women being paired off with them to have sex. As if I was to grant the 'ultimate favour' to some unknown ocker Aussie. The proposition was an abomination for a woman of my refinement, my background, my education. 'It's an outrage,' I yelled at him. 'I can't abide being married to you and soon I shall leave you.' This only prompted the usual comments from him: 'You horrible little English prude.'; 'You stuck-up pommy bitch.'; 'You need to see a doctor as you are frigid.'; and the classic, 'You really have got tickets on yourself.' I was well used to them by now and sought solace in knowing that soon I would be able to leave him and forget that I ever knew him. It was just as well that I refused Graham's proposal, as later on an acquaintance of ours called Jane became heavily involved in this very group; she soon turned to drink, before eventually driving out to a desolate region of the outback, where she knew no one would find her to stop her, and killing herself.

Once his mother Effie came round and I told her to control her son and have a word with him as I wasn't going to tolerate him much longer. 'I am going to divorce him as soon as I can,' I told her. 'I would do it now but I cannot abandon my mother and have to remain in Melbourne while Stefan is alive but as soon he dies, we shall be off.' Effie's bottom lip used to quiver when she was lost for words and her bottom dentures wobbled. She thought the sun shone out of her son and I that was lucky to have him.

One night he hit me severely for refusing him, having had too much to drink, and I ran for refuge in the bathroom. He came after me and punched the door with his fist making quite a dent in it as it was not solid wood. I went to the local doctor the next day to show him my black eye and make a report for future divorce proceedings and the GP instructed me to write the date above the hole in the door and photograph it. There was no point in reporting him to the police for assault as they regarded that as a 'domestic'. I told him how very worried I was about my mother and asked what we were to expect with Stefan's brain tumour. How will it progress and what sort of nursing will he need? The doctor looked at me blankly and said that Stefan didn't have a brain tumour at all; 'Whatever made you think such a ridiculous thing? You are not to worry yourself as all that is the matter with Stefan is that he drinks too much.' So it was then that it dawned on me that my mother had been lying. By now I hardly knew what to believe or who to trust. However, the doctor told me that the drinking had to stop or he would certainly die of cirrhosis of the liver. Whilst I was there speaking routinely of my periods we realised that I was pregnant again. I was shocked as I'd been having sex so rarely and besides, I had tried to keep within the safe period. I must have got my dates confused. But after letting it sink in, I welcomed this new pregnancy as it meant I was making little human beings and would have a family to love and love me back. I also thought that, seeing as we were to be stuck in Australia for about a year waiting for Stefan's death, this new baby would at least give my mother something to look forward to. I hoped it might be a girl and I could call her Camilla as I had promised, although I had quite gone off my mother by now.

Then came the terrible day when I had my first ever row with my mother. I was about three months pregnant and spending the day with her sitting in her kitchen chatting idly. I casually mentioned that, though I was sure the baby would be a girl, if it was a boy I would name him Tadeusz, after my grandfather. My mother became incandescent with rage and screamed at me for the first time in her life; I had never seen her face so distorted and twisted with anger. She insisted that if the child was a boy, I had to call him Stefan, as that would portray her in a good light. And besides she didn't want to be constantly reminded of my grandfather, as she despised heroes and hated my lifelong devotion to him. Then she said she would much rather the baby died than be called Tadeusz. I completely fell to bits. I sobbed hysterically as she then yelled at me that she had only come to Australia to be with me and that it was all my fault that she was so lonely now. The barrage of verbal abuse was of such unexpected intensity that I began trembling and was at the point of fainting with shock. I remember her angrily giving me a glass of whisky to pull me together, which I waved away crying. She insisted that I drink it and when I refused she shouted and tormented me mercilessly, saying the vilest and cruellest things about how she wanted my baby dead and she hoped I would die in childbirth too as I had ruined her life. I hardly remember how I wobbled back home; I walked in the heat with tears streaming down my face and my head spinning and throbbing. A couple of times I had to stop and lean against a tree as my legs were buckling.

When Graham came home I think he was horrified by the distressed state he found me in but didn't understand the enormity of what had happened. I dare say I was a gibbering wreck and I lay on my bed inconsolable. I never got over that afternoon's tirade; it was etched on my memory forever and from then on I saw my mother in a stark light, realising how spiteful and manipulative she was. She had taken such malicious pleasure in upsetting me that from that day forwards I put up an impenetrable barrier between us; I had loved her once as a child but now she was a horrid, sick adult with little merit or good character. The next day she turned up at my front door with a guilty look on her face, carrying an ornamental brass pot as a conciliatory gift. I looked at her with icy silence and simmering hatred. Little did I know that worse was to come.

Chapter 8

I was to stay in Australia for another three years, during which time my mother became a total wreck, drinking and smoking on a path of self-destruction. Stefan, too, was in sharp decline, totally housebound and never seen without his oriental navy satin dressing gown on. I confronted my mother as to why she had lied to me about the brain tumour and she shrugged indifferently. I felt overwhelmed with responsibilities, having become her carer and also to a certain extent Stefan's, since my mother was constantly burdening me with details of his health. She continually asked me to go to the doctors on her behalf and ask if there was any way Stefan's death could be hurried along. When we went out she would frequently fall over drunkenly. She became such a hypochondriac she ordered a taxi to take her to the doctors every week, repeatedly coming away with boxes of tranquilisers and antidepressants which coupled with her drinking made her a ruin of a woman. I didn't grow to hate her with a vengeful, angry attitude but with deep, sad resignation instead, as I realised that they were like two millstones around my neck. All my hopes for the future were thwarted and my trust destroyed. There was an occasion when my mother came to my house and told me Stefan was threatening her with a knife. I rang the doctor and begged him to come and give him an injection of something before he stabbed my mother but the doctor refused, saying, 'but he might stab me.'

I couldn't help but have some compassion, as Mum and Stefan had no friends and nothing to do. Once I was invited to a BBQ by a nice girl called Sue who lived far away in a lovely, old suburb called Mount Waverley. She had a baby the same age as mine and we had met when I was at the aftercare home. I took my mother with me to give her some pleasure, as I still felt it was my duty to take her out but as could be expected, she drank far too much. We were all sitting in a group under a shady tree in pleasant circumstances and company when she pulled a handkerchief out of her handbag. To my dismay the hankie was wrapped around about ten pills; blue ones, red and yellow ones and all sorts. She proceeded to swallow them in front of all the guests and within minutes she was not making any sense at all. The people there were speechless and exchanged glances full of raised eyebrows and mockery.

Stefan had been left at home because he was too drunk to get out of bed. Their house had become a dark, gloomy, cursed place and I very rarely went there as I couldn't bear it. No one ever called except the grocery delivery man and occasionally Graham, who went over some evenings when the three of them would polish off a flagon of sherry. I would always be pleased to be left in peace. I only went there when absolutely necessary and when I did, Stefan would be habitually seated on a stool, propped up against the kitchen worktop, drinking constantly. He would sit wearing his dirty dressing gown, which usually parted to show an expanse of bare leg covered in dark varicose veins. We never spoke and my mother once told me that he used the word 'vermin' in reference to my baby.

I was pregnant, always at home with a mountain of housework and a small child. I didn't particularly want to see my mother much but I routinely rang her every lunchtime out of duty. She would often crossly say that I was only ringing her because I thought I had to, which was true. We made desultory conversation and we had nothing to say to each other; it was all very detached and emotionless and I was relieved when each chat finished and the telephone receiver was sadly placed on its hook. My mother's nearest neighbours were Mr and Mrs Lambert. They had built a lovely house for their retirement and Mrs Lambert, a grey-haired, scraggy, skinny woman in glasses would always be seen tending her garden. Mr

Lambert however had noticed my mother and they began an affair. Once I went to my mother's house whilst Stefan was on one of his regular drying-out phases in hospital. The back door, usually left open, was closed, so I let myself through the garden gate to peek into her bedroom window and see if she was asleep or drunk or whatever. Instead, I saw her on her bed having sex with Mr Lambert. As they all lived so close, it was only a matter of time before Mrs Lambert cottoned on. She and my mother traded angry words and then they sold their pretty house and moved away. Honestly, I thought to myself, is no man safe from her tomfoolery? And it's not as though Mr Lambert was particularly handsome; I thought he was a grinning oaf but I understood how desperately bored she was to resort to such measures.

I had nobody to confide in as Graham wasn't interested in my problems. He accepted my pregnancy with a shrug, he was neither pleased nor displeased; I don't even think he asked when it was due. Effie wasn't in the slightest bit interested by the pregnancy; it was just another encumbrance that I was saddling poor Graham with. She felt I was chaining him to me and continued to tell him at every opportunity that he should have married 'a nice Australian girl', whereas I considered him to be the yoke that oppressed and shackled me but she didn't get it. I had no one to form a bond with, no human connections to survive as a social animal and I became introverted and found life unimaginably hard.

Graham drove me to the market on Saturday mornings and we did our weekly shopping but I heard from the old farmer Cyril, who had the land behind ours, that there were plans for a Safeway to be built by Macedon Square and that would make life easier as I could walk there. Also there would soon be a motorway to the city which would cut travelling time in half. On the first Wednesday of each month a mobile library would come to our district in a large van and I looked forward to it. Whatever the weather I would push my pram and hurry to get a good selection of books.

Mother Anguish

I devoured history text books mainly as they were escapism. I read factual books and also historical novels, losing myself in the Poldark stories and others.

Graham would always be out drinking with the lads on a Friday and occasionally during the week he would come home around midnight. Once he was out with two mates Ron and Matt who had had an argument and fallen out badly. Graham, who was the least drunk, was giving them a lift home. Matt was sitting in the backseat furious about something and had then apparently tried to strangle Ron in the front passenger seat. I was woken up by a commotion in the hallway and jumping out of bed I saw Graham bringing in this man Matt, who I had never met before. 'Whatever's going on? It's the middle of the night,' I said and Graham explained that Matt was dangerous and had tried to kill Ron. Therefore, he told me, he had brought him back to our house while he drove Ron home and would be returning to get Matt in about half an hour. He had to separate them or they would kill each other. 'You can't leave me alone with a drunken and dangerous stranger,' I protested, 'I've got a small child and I'm pregnant,' to which Graham replied, 'He won't want to kill you. He just wants to kill Ron and he is not a stranger, he is one of the staff from work.' I couldn't go back to bed as I was too nervous with that man in the house so I sat grimly with my arms folded. It was especially perilous as I had no panic alarm in the house, or indeed anything for my security. I considered ringing the police but as he was semi-comatose on the sofa, I just watched him cautiously, not taking my eyes of him for a minute. I certainly didn't offer him any coffee or water as I was furious; I didn't even speak to him as he sat on the sofa with his head leaning backwards. After a while Matt vomited on my sitting room floor and I thought 'filthy pig' but took some satisfaction in knowing that Graham would have the job of cleaning it up, which he did when he returned at about 3 a.m. I went to bed exhausted, thinking with abhorrence and revulsion that responsible married men do not as a rule inflict dangerous, drunken strangers on to their pregnant wives.

Melbourne winters are surprisingly cold, with dark skies and persistent rain, although it never snows. As with much of the southern hemisphere, there is a biting wind that blows from the Antarctic. Everyone agrees that it's a different damp cold that gets right into a person's marrow; it is totally unlike the European winters which are freezing but dry. My house was incredibly chilly as not only was it was built on a high hill but it was also raised above the ground by stilts, leaving four feet of empty air beneath at the mercy of the gusting wind. The wooden floor was icy as it was only one-inch thick with no carpet and there was no heating apart from a two-bar electric heater which I carried around from room to room. I occasionally put all the gas on in the kitchen. I put draft excluders beneath every door. We never used the sitting room with its open fire as it was too large a room to warm up; instead we sat in the small TV room which was snug so long as you kept the door shut. But sooner or later we had to go to bed and walk down the freezing corridor. We wore coats in the house at all times. These were the days before everybody lived in warm leggings and cosy fleeces. In the mornings the windows were wet on the inside and I smudged my fingers on the panes of glass in our bedroom in disbelief. The baby always had a cough and a runny nose and I used to take him into my bed at night sometimes to keep him warm; we had an electric blanket of course and I had bought the baby a little one for his own cot but I couldn't leave it on whilst he was sleeping alone in case he wet himself in the night and electrocuted himself or something. As it is he always had a cold blue runny nose each morning and I spent my running away fund buying extra heaters, including one in his room which I warned him never to touch. I couldn't get my washing dry so I told Graham I was going to buy a heated towel rail and he even objected to that as he considered it 'decadent'.

Mother Anguish

I resented Effie for living in her cosy solid brick house in East Malvern with heating and thick fitted carpets. After Garnet's death she had more than enough money to cater for her needs but she point-blank refused to lend us any so that we could put in central heating. I could never understand her total disregard for her only grandchild's health and welfare. She spent freely on new clothes for herself, endless twinsets and matching tweed skirts, and on trips to the hairdressers, where her hair was made bluer and bluer. She would zoom around shopping in her little white car, enjoying unrestricted widowhood. Garnet's name was never ever mentioned; it was as though he had never existed, despite her having been married to him for thirty years. The rest of the time she seemed away with the fairies due to her Valium consumption.

She did, however, continue with her knitting and produced a number of lovely little babies' jumpers of pure wool. I was grateful but told her I would much prefer it if she could perhaps buy some warm all-in-one Babygro suits for him, as woollen jumpers would shrink however carefully I hand-washed them; they were pretty but not practical and I was always washing as Adam constantly dribbled. However, knitting was her hobby so anything else I said fell on deaf ears. She merely enjoyed producing tiny garments.

There was no point in asking my mother or Stefan for a loan, despite them having plenty of money which they had deposited in a high-interest account to provide them with an income. Moreover my mother was so bitter about being in Melbourne that whenever I mentioned the cold she would lurch into unreasonable quarrels with me, complaining how her life was ruined because of my having gone there in the first place. She had no sympathy for my plight. I am certain that Graham must have been suffering in the cold house as well and I frequently told him that surely he could afford to install heating now that he had fifty-one per cent of the business, which was then making money. But he replied that any profits the business made had to be ploughed back in to make more profit. I suspect that he sadistically enjoyed having me at such a disadvantage as when I finally left him years later, he promptly installed central heating and also built a swimming pool and all manner of comforts.

One very cold day I took a basket of nappies to hang out behind the house to dry. Graham flew into a rage at the thought of disposable nappies and wouldn't even have Kleenex tissues in the house in the interests of economy; he always used disgusting handkerchiefs and I never understood how he could blow his nose into a cloth, wrap it up like a piece of treasure and then put it back in his pocket. Graham always left his outdoor boots by the backdoor so I slipped my feet into them as I didn't want to get my slippers dirty and then proceeded to yomp through the mud. I was too much of a snob to have a rotary hoist in the middle of the back yard and so walked the small distance to where I had a clothes line by the outer fence. Having pegged out the washing, I returned, sat on the back step and took his shoes off to leave in their place. As I shook out one of his shoes, a huge dead tarantula spider fell out, its legs all curled up under its big hairy body; it had obviously sought shelter there and perished. I remember sitting on those steps with my head in my hands thinking, 'Oh God, what has become of me? Where is the girl that went to Queen's Club, shopped in Harrods, had her hair done at Vidal Sassoon's salon in Sloane Street and was driven around in E-Type jaguars by men in three-piece suits?' Here I was with flimsy socks on my feet, hugely pregnant and with a small, sickly child to care for; a drunken, violent husband; a drunken, aggressive mother; and in addition, an invalid stepfather. We were all living together in wretchedness in a hideous area with no mature trees to act as a windbreak and, as if that wasn't bad enough, I had just spent twenty minutes with a fucking great dead spider in my shoe right at the end of my toes, the flesh of which was coloured purple by chilblains which had reignited from my school days. I was absolutely terrified, a ghost of my confident seventeen-year-old self. I was completely beaten down with creeping misery and had hit rock bottom. I was not, however, tempted to give way to self-pity and end up remaining there for the term of my natural life; it only made me angry with myself and determined to escape or die in the attempt.

I cursed myself for letting Graham persuade me into living in the Templestowe area. Designing the house had been a diversion but I would have so much preferred to have bought a solid brick house in an old suburb with an established, lush garden. And maybe I would have had some neighbours to pass the time of day with. And some shops around the corner to nip to for pleasure. We couldn't afford East Malvern but there were some dinky, old houses in nearby Ashburton. Graham had argued that he didn't want a 'second-hand house' and insisted that this was just the way things were done in Australia, buying a plot of land and building a new house for yourself.

Gradually more houses started to be built in our area but they were not as decorative as ours. Endless ticky-tacky bungalows appeared far off near Dandenong hills; run-of-the-mill cream brick veneer dwellings with flat roofs. My beautiful house, which I had designed with such hope and artistry, looked completely incongruous in its surroundings, standing white and tall like a tombstone. Once I saw it from a couple of miles away and it made me think of a flower on a dung heap. Graham had been totally wrong in his prediction that Templestowe would be the new Toorak. It was a dump. As our house was built on a high vantage point I could see for miles all around; a perfect spot to witness our environs' gradual transformation into a panorama of bleak, treeless suburbia. The ugly new-build houses that continued to spring up also looked like tombstones. I was living out my life in a dismal, desolate uncultivated wasteland. This was the cemetery of my time on earth and I deserved better.

My chief preoccupation was waiting each day for the postman. Knowing that the amount of letters one receives is commensurate with the amount one sends out, I wrote endlessly to my friends in England. My friends in London were a lazy lot, enjoying life, but nevertheless took pity occasionally and wrote me long, gossipy pages with all the news I yearned for. The postman used to come by motorbike at around 11 a.m. and I could hear him from a great distance. I watched anxiously from my window as he approached the house and prayed that he would stop his motor and slip some post into the letterbox which stood at the bottom of my drive. I was inconsolable if he just drove past, as it meant another empty day ahead, but if I saw him stop I would scurry down and look desperately to see if there was blue airmail envelope and if one appeared then my heart would leap with joy. Oh, the joy to receive news from London!

Graham capitalised on my vulnerability as he knew now that I was well and truly stuck. He laughed, together with everybody else, at my previous exalted London lifestyle, which I had described at length, giving myself all manner of airs and graces. I think to some extent he revelled in cutting me down to size after the inadequacy he had felt when amongst my urbane and sophisticated London friends. They had taken every opportunity to turn their noses up at him for being an ocker Aussie and now that he had this 'stuck-up, pommy bitch' as an outsider in his own domain, he wasted no time in avenging that previous emasculation. He was especially confident in mocking me now that my mother was not the glamorous bombshell I had painted her to be. The reality was that she had drunkenly let herself go. Before I had always spoken of her with pride as being so very charming and of my stepfather as a successful businessman and suddenly here were these two embarrassing Polacks. As much as foreigners were looked down upon in England it was a hundred times worse in Australia. But even though I hated my mother I still felt a sense of responsibility for her and couldn't leave her in such a condition.

Mother Anguish

Graham went to the city every day but when he came home he complained that I hadn't done enough housework and would wipe his finger over shelves looking for dust. One day he said to me, 'If you want to please me, my dinner must be ready when I come home,' and I looked at him in disbelief. Didn't he realise that I had by then no inclination to please him in any way? I also wondered what had happened to the cheerful, handsome surfer who I had met in Spain; he now had a jowly, florid face from guzzling three large bottles of beer every night and had grown a hideous gut. This was made worse by his habit of drinking a mixture of port and brandy all weekend long and having a drunken nap in the afternoons only to wake up and start drinking again.

I did cook in those days but it was just a case of putting a leg of lamb into the oven, surrounded by potatoes and pumpkins just like Effie used to do. I liked roast lamb anyway and it always provided a lovely, juicy leg bone for my dog Gabby to chew on. One day Graham decided that I hadn't cleaned the oven well enough, which was a difficult task if I cooked a spluttering roast nearly every day. He actually grabbed me by the ear and pulled me across the kitchen, sticking my head into the oven as he snarled to show me that it wasn't thoroughly clean. I lashed out and hit him with all my might and of course he hit me back and swore. I would have scratched him if I could but I had bitten all my fingernails from despair and a complete disinterest in my appearance.

For pudding Graham used to enjoy chocolate mousse and by a stroke of incredibly good luck, I found something called Ex-Lax in the chemist. This was a chocolate-flavoured laxative and I used to doctor his pudding with generous quantities of it. Whenever he complained of having a dodgy stomach I used to say, 'Well, you do drink too much, far too much and it obviously disagrees with you. You must cut down on drinking so much brandy,' and he would reply, 'Aw, shut your neck!' His diarrhoea was my only entertainment and it worked a treat. Not only did he spend less money on alcohol but it also did wonders in suppressing his libido as he spent so much time in the lavatory. Brilliant, I thought to myself and wondered how I hadn't come up with it before.

Even before he hit me I used to try and get our sex over and done with, not allowing for any preceding foreplay or fumbling under any circumstances. But from thence on I refused point-blank to ever let him take his pleasure again. A few times he tried to execute his matrimonial rights by attempting to kiss me. I always turned away but one time he got me; I kept my mouth tightly shut and my body stiffened and in exasperation he screamed at me: 'Kissing you is like kissing a fish's arse!' I knew that my life would have been easier if I had let him have his way occasionally but I couldn't and wouldn't ever again contemplate having sex with him; the very thought made me sick.

To put him in a good mood, however, I would make him his favourite chocolate pudding which he ate with gusto.

One day he came home and announced he was going to buy me a car because he realised how isolated I was. He drove me on a Saturday morning to an outdoor car showroom which was laid out along American lines with bunting and a cheerful atmosphere. I saw a lovely bright yellow Datsun 260Z and Graham asked me if I would like to have it. I couldn't believe my luck and nodded enthusiastically but he then took the wind out of my sails by saying with a stern seriousness, 'If you are good for six months then I will buy you that car.' I was under no illusions about the nature of his proposition; he meant I was to oblige all of his sexual needs. I almost broke down sobbing in the showroom and we returned home silent.

He continued to grumble constantly about me reading books. Whenever he saw me reading he would seethe with inarticulate frustration. I would often settle down to one while eating my favourite snack of toast and cheese with mango chutney, only for him to angrily interrupt, saying, 'There you are, stuffing your mouth, nose in a book again.' I tried to make him realise what a wonderful world there is in books so that it would give him an interest other than drinking. I once recommended that he read *The Godfather* but he found it too complicated. In that respect I tried to be a good wife in the hope that he might become a better husband; for the time I was stuck there we could at least live in some sort of harmony. He enjoyed gardening and created artistic volcanic rock formations in the garden, into which he planted decorative mosses and pretty native Australian flora. I was hoping that we might develop a shared interest of some kind, any kind, as sometimes I felt sorry for him leading a simple and a moronic life but in all the years that I was there we never ever once went to the cinema or the theatre. He didn't seem at all embarrassed by the deficiencies in his education and showed no interest in bettering himself or learning anything. Australia was a complete cultural wasteland and we never ever went out to a restaurant either.

Being pregnant for the second time, I had the regular joy of seeing Professor Leeton again at his practice in the city. Wandering around town, going into the great store Myers and seeing him at our appointments were the only things that kept me sane. As with my previous pregnancy, I developed high blood pressure and pre-eclampsia so the baby had to be brought on a month early in October. Thus, once again there was no dramatic dash to the hospital; Graham drove me there on his way to work, having first stopped at Effie's to drop off my toddler so she could look after him while I was away. Childbirth is not called 'labour' for nothing. Having again refused an epidural, as I still found them creepy, and after an eternity of pain and pushing, I finally delivered a daughter. I must have fainted right at the end as I suddenly heard the words 'Look Basia, look Basia' and saw the tiny, slimy, purply body being held aloft by a smiling Professor Leeton. As with Adam, they took her away to the premature babies ward immediately. The next morning I begged to be allowed to see the baby but the nurses insisted I wait for a wheelchair as she was on a different floor. Eventually I was wheeled down and they brought her cot to the window so I could look at her through the glass. I fell in love instantaneously and sat there gazing for about an hour, enchanted by this tiny scrap of humanity with a little hat on. A girl. I couldn't believe that I finally had my little girl. She was beautiful, fair-haired and blue-eyed, and I named her Camilla. I had a wonderful week in hospital, enjoying the bustle and the cheerful, kindly nurses. I made friends with one of the other new mums, another Sue who subsequently became my best friend, and felt human again away from my mother and Stefan.

When I brought the new baby home I kept her cot right next to my bed and on the first night I was woken by my mother and Stefan coming into the darkened room. They were both drunk but Graham had fetched them in his car to see the baby. Stefan had never once been in my room before. My mother bent over the crib to pick up the child and asked if she could take the baby home with her for a month so that they could look after it while I got some rest. I was dumbstruck with horror at the thought of these two drunks taking away my newborn to play with as if she was some toy. I sat bolt up-right, clasping my precious little bundle to my chest, and firmly said, 'absolutely not.' My mother was very offended.

As soon as I had fully recovered, I decided to take a tough approach to sobering up my mother and Stefan. As talking about her ailments and miseries was her chief hobby, she needed little persuasion to embark on a trip to the Austin Hospital in the nearby suburb of Heidelberg. I made an appointment with a psychiatrist in advance and coaxed her and Stefan into a taxi. I think she was almost looking forward to the novelty of this exciting new excursion. When we got to the reception, however, she started hyperventilating and trembling, possibly over-acting for the benefit of all the medical attention. When I asked her to walk she leant on me heavily and so I deposited them in the waiting room and rushed in advance

Mother Anguish

down the corridor to the doctor, desperately saying, 'Please help me,' before giving him a quick resume of my problem relatives. I was quite relieved when he grasped my situation immediately and briskly took matters into hand, ordering my mother to breathe in and out of a paper bag to stop the hyper attack and finding her a hospital bed to recuperate in. A little while later, as I waited for her to recover, I happened to look at my mother's medical notes at the end of her bed and I noticed a new ailment written down, labelled as 'PFO'. I was alarmed that it might be some serious disease or condition but found out afterwards it stood for 'Pissed Fell Over'. The doctor persuaded them both to agree to a short stay as inmates in the drying-out ward, promising good company and plenty of therapy. It was surprisingly easy and after assuring them of daily visits, I left feeling fairly light-hearted.

Stefan was in a worse state than my mother and I did not know what to expect. In the bed next to him lay a miserable man called Sam Parker who spoke to me at every occasion, complaining that he had no visitors ever and no friends at all. This seemingly innocuous and feeble person later turned out to be an evil man who would cause untold misery in my life for the next twenty-five years. If only I had known this at the time. But he was stranger to me, just a sick old man in a hospital bed and I politely acknowledged him whenever I visited. He was forty-two years old, thin, unemployed and a widower. He said he was an Englishman from Ruislip who had emigrated to Australia some time ago with his wife, before she had died of a cancerous appendix. He possessed a face like a bloodhound, never smiled and grumbled constantly about life and the nurses and said his only pleasure in life was riding his bike when well and talking to Stefan. When Stefan was discharged just before Christmas, I felt so sorry for this lonely man that I insanely invited him to Christmas lunch. He accepted with enthusiasm but arrived on the day with no presents or even bottle of wine. The lunch comprised of Graham and I, Mum and Stefan, both successfully detoxed and looking quite well, Effie and Sam. I roasted a turkey with trimmings, lay a white lace tablecloth, fished out my best antique china crockery, which my mother had brought over from England, and we made the best of it in the sweltering heat, watching the Queen's speech. I bought my mother a new dress and a book for Stefan. I also bought a cheap keyboard and I learnt how to play Christmas songs to amuse everyone.

Sam Parker became a permanent fixture in our lives and turned up at Mum and Stefan's house every single evening without fail for his dinner. My mother always cooked and I suspected he was taking terrible advantage and got quite irritated as he was not contributing anything financially. I also suspected that he was borrowing money as he was unemployed. However, since I had two tiny children to look after, I tried to take the attitude that his company for Mum and Stefan was taking the pressure off me.

One evening Graham and I were going out to dinner at Sue and John's, a pleasant, plodding couple who, just like Jane and Tony, were always boasting of how high their eucalyptus trees had grown in the last year. My mother, being sober, was due to babysit and she asked me not to return home too early as she was planning to invite Sam around to our house and seduce him. I was so tired and fed up with her by now that I didn't object, although I thought her quite demented and warned her to be careful she didn't get herself pregnant, as she'd had a scare four months earlier. We returned home well after midnight and the next day my mother said that she and Sam had had sex in every room but I stonewalled the details as I was so disgusted I didn't want to know. From then on Sam had a triumphant look on his face. He always reminded me of Charles Dickens's Uriah Heep; of very humble demeanour but treacherous, deceitful, conniving, greedy, avaricious and worse. He must have noticed my mother's splendid furniture and being lower middle class there was no way he was going to sever relations now that he was getting sex, food and the chance to replace her dying husband.

Mother Anguish

Stefan had started drinking again and Sam encouraged him. My mother continued her affair with Sam and I sadly reflected on how when a woman gets older, her standards get lower. Sam was definitely sub-standard.

My salvation came one Friday night when Graham was arrested for drink-driving while out with the boys. He had previously admitted to me that every Friday he went to a topless massage parlour and found it wonderful to have a woman's great breasts flopping into his face as she rubbed his chest or whatever. I didn't want the details as I was so disgusted by him. Some nights he didn't come home at all and I was so frightened to be in such an isolated and deserted house with small children, no nearby neighbours and a flimsy front-door lock that I used to lie awake until dawn listening to every sound. On one such night, at the break of daylight, the police brought Graham home in the back of a van. He had been arrested and his car was impounded at the station. He was furious to be without a car as, with distances being so vast in Australia and the city so far away, it was on par with being disabled. His brother Ian picked up Graham's car and brought it to our garage and from that day on Ian would come early each day and drive Graham to work. At Graham's court case the following week he lost his driving licence for a year and I immediately thought to myself that now he couldn't object to me learning to drive. At last I saw a glimmer of freedom. I booked driving lessons immediately and passed my test first time, which is unusual for a woman.

Chapter 9

Having acquired the ability to drive, I could now get a job. As my mother was sober, I asked her to babysit and she agreed with the condition that I paid her for it. I resolved to stop picking at my mosquito bites and make myself pretty again. I scrutinised my face and upon releasing my hair, which I had continuously kept tied back, I realised with some surprise how long it had grown without my noticing. Graham had totally undermined my confidence in my looks but after a trip to the hairdressers for some blonde highlights, I realised that there might be some hope after all as I was quite pleased with the result. So I returned and had some more highlights done; I chucked my glasses into a drawer and got contact lenses; and I bought false eyelashes and applied any artifice available to improve upon what nature had bestowed on me. I remember having read once that an Act of Parliament was almost passed in 1770 to render marriages null and void if the woman had lured her husband into matrimony through the use of false hairpieces and padded bosoms or hips and that always made me laugh. The object of beautifying myself now was not a marriage but a career to advance my future. I tended to my complexion like a precious flower and as soon as my skin had cleared up, I piled on the lipstick and make-up and felt ready to face the world and start a new chapter in life. I had been transformed from a Knightsbridge 'It girl' into a squalid drudge living in the outer bush but now I was on a mission to reverse this change and there would be no stopping me. I felt a supernatural assuredness that I would reclaim my status in London and make a success of my life; I would be accepted by the royal family (although I had given up on marrying

Mother Anguish

Prince Charles by now) and I would go to all the best parties, mix with cultivated people at last and get a house in Sloane Square. A brilliant era of great accomplishments awaited me; after all, I was well born, well educated and destined for better things than living in this hellhole.

That being said, I still felt incredibly timid and terrified while looking for work but was determined to conceal my nerves and put on a good show. One only had to 'act as if', I told myself. Having scanned the telephone directory, I found an agency called Associated Models and tremulously telephoned the boss, an ex-model called Laurie Bourne, who had since become fat and balding and started an agency instead. It didn't deal with high fashion, for which I would have been unsuitable, being too short, but his was the main agency in town for general work and television commercials. Over the phone he was courteous but matter-of-fact and recommended a photographer in St Kilda Road to do some test shots which I would have to show him before he considered putting me on his books. On the day of my photo shoot I was petrified and spent a great deal of time perfecting my hair and make-up. I wore new white jeans and a pale grey T-shirt with a short-sleeved white denim jacket. I also brought a plain white evening dress for variety. The photographer was called Rob and he put me at ease. He took me to a beach jetty for some casual shots and then back to his studio for some glamorous photos. I was delighted to have met such a trendy, cheerful snapper, who made me look so good too.

I nervously took the contact sheets to Laurie Bourne, who studied my photos with a magnifying loop, picked out the best for my z card and said, 'consider us in business as of now.' I returned home in seventh heaven. The very next day he rang me with a job to go to. My very first job! I was to stand in a kitchen set advertising a fridge. The photo appeared in that evening's *Melbourne Herald* newspaper and I was beyond thrilled. Not exactly the cover of *Vogue* but I was being paid $50 an hour. It was riches. A week later

I was cast for a commercial advertising dresses. I was scared stiff, as I had never done catwalk modelling, and went to the agency office to explain my fears but kindly Laurie simply got up from his desk and did a few pirouettes, saying, 'Just do it like this.' I laughed to see this bulky man arranging his legs and feet in dainty poses and my nerves were instantly calmed. It later dawned on me that I looked quite pretty twirling for the cameras in my floral frock, which was made from a delicate pale-pink-and-grey material. That commercial was shown a few times a night for over a week.

'I awoke one morning and found myself famous,' as Byron once famously put it. Everywhere I went the atmosphere was zippy and the film crews so friendly and welcoming; totally unlike any of the people I had mixed with in Australia before. It was a shock to my system that everyone seemed to like me so much. Spontaneous and wholehearted friendship followed me everywhere I went. I had had so many years of Graham belittling me, undermining my looks, criticising everything about me and telling me how much his friends hated me that I felt my personality had been totally dismantled and eroded. Whenever his unkind words and insults had provoked a response, he would use my reaction to tell me I was crazy. Now, out of the blue, I was much in demand and on television every night, sometimes for a small segment and other times as the star. At one stage I was appearing in three different commercials simultaneously, with the set fee for a starring role usually being in the thousands of dollars and an appearance amongst co-stars in the hundreds. The going rate for photographic modelling was $100 an hour.

These trendy, wonderful people from my glamorous new life had no idea that I lived in far-off Templestowe and they might have laughed if I'd told them. After a job we would invariably take ourselves to a wine bar and discuss the day's events with laughter and camaraderie. In all my time in Melbourne I had never set foot in any wine bar or coffee bar even. There was bonhomie all around and I revelled in having found at last a cheerful sense of belonging. They always complimented me and said how much they were looking forward to working with me again and then I would bid them a fond farewell with hugs and drive off, often into the sunset, with the radio blaring songs from *Evita*.

Effie and Graham must have been speechless with astonishment but the balance of power had shifted so much that I didn't even discuss it with them. Effie once commented that she had been watching television and thought to herself, 'Oh my God, there she is again,' but she never uttered a word of pride or praise. Indeed, my new circumstances only elicited complaints from her over a perceived dereliction of duty in the housework department. I would have smirked if congratulations had been forthcoming; they had devoted so many years to isolating me from the world that I knew my success was a disaster to their plans and efforts to control me. It must have been very hard for them to accept this metamorphosis while routinely sitting at Effie's dinner table. For years they had had there a sullen, resentful girl with scraped-back hair in a rubber band, a spotty face, ravaged fingernails, glasses and no make-up but almost overnight I had transformed into one with flowing blonde hair and immaculate make-up and clothes, who graced the television each evening with a smile on her face.

I now regarded Graham casually, as an inconsequential encumbrance rather than a serious threat, and it must have dawned on him that he had become merely an appendage to a more impressive and famous spouse. No one wanted him around and he wasn't needed in any way. One evening as filming was running late on a commercial for Kraft, a company that makes healthy cheeses, the chairman of the firm came to watch its progress with a couple of his friends and they all stood around at the back of the room. Camilla was now a beautiful blonde toddler and we were cast as a mother and daughter duo. It was very hot and we had to do take after take, as on this occasion I was nervous and my movements and words got muddled up a few times. At this point Graham turned up and headed towards the set, ostensibly to see if I was all right as there was no other reason for him to be there; he couldn't say he was driving me home because he still was without a licence. I think he was mostly there just to establish himself as my husband as he was starting to get jealous. Embarrassingly, he interrupted the director in the middle of a take, saying something banal about having seen him and me doing a different commercial sometime before, and he was rewarded with a very impatient look and told to move and not stand in the way. To my satisfaction he had made a fool of himself and I glanced at him as if he was a dreadful nuisance, waving him away with a carefully manicured hand. I had stopped biting my fingernails by now.

My daughter Camilla, now aged two, was cheerful and funny and we were often booked for mother-daughter TV commercials for fabric softener etc. She was very bright and took instruction from the directors like a natural-born actress. She then did a couple of commercials all by herself; one for the milk marketing board and one for dog food, where she was filmed playing with and hugging a dog as I stood aside watching with bursting pride. At that age she wasn't paid much so I always bought her a new doll or pretty dress.

I felt like an alpha female at full strength and I gloried in my spectacular good fortune and the astonishing turn of the wheel. A large store called Buckley's in Collins Street decided to use me as their permanent hat model. Even Laurie Bourne said I had a splendid head for hats; he once told me that 'one could put a cow pat on your head and it would look good'. Buckley's had the whole right-hand column of the *Melbourne Herald* and advertised in each edition, so my face was on the front page daily. What delicious revenge. And it was all well-paid work. Soon I would have earnt enough to escape.

Jobs would usually take place in the morning when I had one child at school and another at kindergarten or at my mother's, so I could pick and choose my work and be home at the end of the school day. I even got a bit part in the iconic show *The Sullivans*, Australia's answer to *Coronation Street*. The producers had seen me in an advert on television and decided they liked my high cheekbones; they said I had a '1930s face' which was just right for their period drama set in wartime Melbourne. In my scene I was to portray an elegant lady at the Melbourne Cup, Australia's equivalent to Ascot. They dressed me to perfection and I played my part with aplomb. Everyone was delighted and I was very well paid. The money was now rolling in and I saved every penny for my England fund. I spent my nights calculating my savings and decided I had enough by now to buy a little house in Fulham or Battersea, which I had heard was an up-and-coming area where property values would continue to rise. Alternatively, if I could face living with my mother and she stayed sober, then we could pool our resources and buy a place in Knightsbridge.

My son Adam was always sickly and caught no end of southern-hemisphere viruses. I was told he needed to have his tonsils out and having faith in the medical profession, I foolishly agreed. I handed him over to a small local hospital called Bellbird for what I thought would be a routine minor procedure and instead it nearly killed him. I was told to telephone at 7 p.m. to enquire on his progress but when I did I heard nurses in the background saying 'It's the mother, it's the mother!' and something muffled about him bleeding to death. My heart started pounding and my mouth went dry and I pressed the receiver as hard as I could to my ear and shouted. Graham heard me yell and came up to me to ask if everything was all right and I screamed at him 'No!' A senior nurse came on to the phone and said there was a slight problem but that the doctor was returning to take Adam back into the theatre. I was not to come to the hospital as they would ring me later. 'I have heard all that's been said,' I shouted at her. 'What's going on? I am coming straight over.' She replied, 'He's oozing a bit,' but would give me no more information.

I drove like a madwoman through red traffic lights, sounding my horn in panic. At one stage I had to stop but my whole body was trembling so much that when I put my shaking foot on to the brake pedal, I found it hard to hold down and the car lurched and jerked before haphazardly coming to a halt. I ran into the hospital and the reception was deserted with no one at the desk. I looked around and saw something vaguely familiar scrunched up in a plastic bag. On closer inspection I recognised it as his new pyjamas, which I had bought him for the hospital 'adventure'. I pulled them out of the bag and they were discoloured with blood and completely dripping with water. Someone had tried washing them without success and then bunged them into the bag for me soaking wet. I dashed down a corridor, not knowing where I was going and flinging open every door I passed. I finally entered a room where my little son was lying unconscious on a bench. He was tipped upwards with two nurses on either side of him, one of whom was wearing a blood-soaked apron. 'What the hell is happening?' I shrieked and they ordered me out, saying the doctor would be there in a minute and if I made too much of a fuss they would call the police. They told me the 'blood was on its way from the city'. 'What are you talking about?' I yelled furiously and they explained that they did not keep stocks of blood for transfusions on the premises and had needed to ring the general hospital in the city, which was rushing it over by ambulance. I sat all alone in the waiting room for I don't know how long. Eventually the specialist approached me with an idiotic, patronising smile on his face and said, 'We nearly lost him,' as if I was supposed to be grateful. He explained that in removing the child's adenoids he had been 'working in a blind area' and as a result had made an incision too deep, causing the near-fatal haemorrhage.

He needed more transfusions and stayed in hospital for another two days. I wanted to sleep by the side of his bed but they wouldn't allow me to stay the night. The next day I saw another batch of little children in the same ward, all of them due to have their tonsils out as well. They were all excited and leaping about on their beds and I was even more furious that my child had to stay in a noisy room with all this commotion while he was ill and on a drip. I had promised my little boy that this trip to the hospital would be a treat to make him better, followed by lots of ice cream and jelly and I shall never forget the accusatory expression his sad eyes took on when I visited him; his judgemental gaze told me he had lost all confidence in his mother. Adam instinctively knew he had been close to death and as I sat by his bed he said to me, very quietly, 'When I am better, can we go away to a beautiful country? Can we go to Scotland?' It was such an odd thing for a four-year-old to say, as I had had no recollection of ever telling him about Scotland but maybe he had seen it on the television. I was young and naive then but I have never trusted the medical profession since. And furthermore, I have read that thousands of people have died worldwide from having their tonsils out but no one has ever died from tonsillitis.

One day soon after, I noticed my little son was limping and looking very ill. I took him to A&E, where they X-rayed his hips and informed me he had Perthes' disease in his left hip. 'He's got what?' I asked in shock, having never heard of such a thing, and they explained to me that it is a degenerative condition affecting the top of the femur, the ball of which crumbles. The only treatment is total immobility with no weight whatsoever being put on the leg. They admitted him to hospital and he spent a month with his leg high in traction. I was beside myself with worry but at least I had a car and could drive there to visit him as often as I wanted. When he was discharged I was told by the doctor that under no circumstances was he allowed to stand on that leg and that he had to spend a full year on crutches holding it up; it was a solemn moment for me to be given the crutches and told I had a crippled child. Adam then proceeded to struggle down the stairs of the hospital on the way out while I slowly guided him with great care. I received a few sympathetic looks from whoever was around but did not smile or acknowledge anyone. However, Adam adapted to using them very quickly and would swing his little body quite fast as he moved along. In the dead of night, whenever he wanted to go to the lavatory, I would listen broken-heartedly to the sound of the crutches and his one leg touching the wooden floor as he clumped along the corridor. Thump, clunk, it sounded. The noise used to wake me and I would get up and rush to help him.

These dreadful misfortunes were used as an excuse for my mother and Stefan to resume drinking, even though Stefan had never shown any interest or affection for the child. I had kept all news of the tonsillectomy emergency away from my mother, as I didn't want her to worry but when the doctors told me Adam was safe, I was so happy that I went to my mother beaming with relief and happiness and told her what had happened. She immediately started yelling, 'Oh my God, Oh my God,' and dived into her larder where I knew she kept her whisky. I pleaded with her, 'Oh please, please don't drink,' but she gulped the whisky straight from the bottle and I was so cross with myself for saying anything. She became very drunk after that. Stefan's liver started to fail and he turned bright yellow, while the whites of his eyes became orange. His stomach grew to enormous proportions and his legs were like sticks. I could not bear going over to that house but realised that my mother had an enormous burden in nursing him in the night-time and keeping him clean. Whenever I saw her she used to say that I had no idea just how ill he was and I would impatiently reply, 'Just stop drinking, for heaven's sake!' I had lost patience with them both.

One morning my mother rang unexpectedly and desperately asked me to drive Stefan to the hospital. Even for the two of us holding him it was a great effort getting him out of bed, wheezing and groaning, through the front door and then squeezing him into the back seat of the car. He was very weak. I had been so busy with my little family and career that I hadn't realised the terrible extent of his deterioration. He asked me for some cigarettes and I drove to the local milk bar and bought him some, actually feeling rather sorry for him. I lit one for him and handed it over but after a couple of puffs he didn't want it. At the hospital I parked a distance away and left my mother, children and Stefan in the car while I went looking for a wheelchair and told the admitting staff that I had an ill man in the car park. They were very helpful but I was reprimanded severely for bringing him in the car; 'this was an ambulance case,' I was told impatiently. Getting him out of the back proved very troublesome indeed as a result of his distended stomach and lack of strength due to muscle wastage. Eventually they managed it and placed him on a stretcher. It was drizzling that day and we must have made a funny procession through the car park, with Stefan wheeled along on a stretcher followed by my mother drunkenly staggering, little Camilla wearing an eye patch, as she had poked herself there a couple of days earlier, and my little son Adam on crutches. And to complete the fancy-dress theme, I was all made-up and in a cocktail frock, as I was supposed to be at a commercial shoot advertising pianos in a couple of hours.

Stefan died a week later. We visited him every day but he made no improvement. I was ignorant of how liver failure progressed and late one evening when the hospital rang to say 'he isn't responding to the treatment', I didn't know that that was a medical euphemism for dying. I drove my mother to the hospital, leaving Graham with the children. Stefan looked dreadful; waxy and dark yellow, his face merely a skull covered in skin with no underlying flesh in his cheeks. They had taken his dentures out and he was very self-conscious; despite being moments from death, he still tried to keep up appearances by putting his hand over his mouth as he whispered. His voice was all thin and reedy and we couldn't understand what he was saying. There was a bright lamp hanging from the ceiling above his head and he asked me to turn it off. I said that I was so sorry but I didn't know how to do it as it was a ceiling light and, typically irrational, he snapped at me, saying, 'You switched it on so you can switch it off.' Thus I was unable to make his final moments easier. I have heard it said that people die as they had lived: calm people die calmly, good-natured people die good-naturedly and hysterical people die ranting. Stefan was bad-tempered right up to the end. The priest came, gave him the last rights, anointing all his seven points with holy oil, and then left. My mother and I sat with him for some time before all of a sudden from his mouth exploded a great gush of bloody vomit, which poured over his bare, swollen stomach like a wide river. My mother and I jumped backwards in shock. Stefan had had a massive internal haemorrhage, which had released itself at the moment of his death. It was a terrible sight to see his face with the blood still trickling and his eyes wide open as if in surprise. I put my arm around my mother saying, 'Don't look Mummy, please don't look.' We went into the corridor and Sam was standing there looking speculative and creepy. He offered to drive my mother to her house so I drove home by myself. Before that, as I walked alone down the hospital corridor I met a doctor who I recognised from a previous visit. I shook as I told him of what I had just witnessed and he said, 'Oh, they all die like that when it's alcoholic liver failure. The liver is the filter of the body and when it stops working the blood banks up and finally explodes with great force.' 'I wish someone had told me that before I came,' I said sombrely, 'I am never going to be the same after seeing something like that.'

Having born witness as my enemy died, I experienced a humbling sense of spiritual responsibility. There was no rejoicing; it was a hollow victory and it made me melancholy. It was Halloween night and as I drove home, I saw cheerful illuminated pumpkins by the roadside. When I stopped at the traffic lights a man tried to get my attention flirtatiously in the next car. I stared back at him with hatred, so angry that he was trying his luck while I had just witnessed the life-altering, dreadful spectacle. I had seen death for the first time at the age of twenty-three and it would be tattooed on my memory forever.

The next day I went very early to my mother's house to find her vomiting in the kitchen sink over and over. I begged her to have some toast and butter for breakfast but she reached for the sherry bottle instead and sat helplessly in a deep armchair, saying, 'I want him back.' Realising that she was deranged I deliberately overlooked the irony of these words, coming as they did after many years of her maintaining a desire for his death. I left her with Sam while I went to the undertakers to make arrangements for the funeral. No one came with me; Graham went to work as normal, totally unaffected and probably relieved that at least one problem was over. He had been exasperated during the last two years at witnessing my anxiety for my mother's wretched circumstances and by my constant weeping with distress as her attitude changed towards me and drink destroyed her looks. They had already collected Stefan's body from the hospital and I asked to see him. 'No, no,' said the mortician, 'he's a dreadful state and you are far too young to see such a thing.' 'Nothing could be worse than last night,' I said, having watched him die. I was taken to a single room where Stefan's dead body lay in a coffin and I walked in very slowly and solemnly with my hands clenched. 'Oh, poor Stefan,' I said with genuine feeling, totally forgetting all the years of animosity. Overnight he had shrunk and dried up into a tiny desiccated husk, a sunken waxy face with no teeth. I touched his cold hand briefly and then told the undertaker to put Stefan's dentures in to give some structure to his face and to comb his hair back, as I didn't want my mother to see him in such a condition. I was suddenly made aware of the futility of feuds and wars. We all have our allotted lifespan; death ultimately comes to us all and we shall all end up equal, dried up and in a box.

Sam moved in on my mother immediately and stayed there. I accepted the situation, thinking that it was best for her not to be alone on that first night. As she was in no state to cook, I went home and made my speciality; macaroni cheese with sliced tomatoes and a cheesy, crispy topping. Being an Englishman, I thought it would be a treat for Sam as well. I took it over there proudly but the next day my mother sneered at me and told me that they both said it was the most disgusting thing they had ever tasted. They had thrown it into the garden and 'even the birds didn't want to eat it'. I confess I was hurt as everyone else, including Graham, always raved about it. This was an early warning of Sam's malign influence over my mother and my instincts were sharpened from thence on as I noticed his gradual seizing of power.

I accepted fewer modelling jobs. I had so much to do at home with both my children ill; one with Perthes' disease and the other an injured eye. Graham was as demanding as ever, trying to assert himself but I took no notice. The house was a mess and my dog Gabby had just had puppies, which I kept in a large basket by my side of the bed. It was very comforting to hear them snuffling and squeaking in the night and I would occasionally get up and attach them in an orderly line to her teats for feeding and gaze at the beautiful little still-blind creatures. I loved picking them up and smelling them, a marvellous scent of mother's milk and biscuits, while Gabby would observe me with trusting eyes.

Stefan's funeral took place quietly with no weeping and then he was buried on Templestowe Hill. I felt a quiet sympathy for the man; he had been born in faraway Poland and once possessed an enchanted, glamorous life in England, residing in the beautiful stucco-fronted Elvaston Place, within walking distance of Kensington Gardens, and driving the latest-model Jaguar car, but his days had come to such a sorry end, being buried in this godforsaken place for all eternity. My mother installed a fine marble slab, sealing him into the bowels of this bleak landscape and I knew now that within a short time, she, I and the children would return to England.

Stefan had died a few weeks before Christmas, which was always an emotionally difficult hurdle, and I thought that my mother was in need of civilising before we went back to the glamorous world of London society. She had to some extent 'gone native' within the confines of the bush and needed restarting. I had by then earnt a great deal of money, all safely deposited in my running away fund, and for this purpose I decided to take some out and pay for her to go on a month-long cruise around the South Pacific and spare her the gruesomeness of Christmas in Melbourne. I thought that she would meet some lively people there and be removed from Sam's pernicious grasp. He had started to treat her house as his own very soon after Stefan's death and on a couple of occasions had invited a man he met from the cycling club to come over and spend the evening. I bought her some pretty clothes and had no doubt that in no time at all she would return to the woman she once was. She was thrilled to be going on the cruise and enjoyed trying on her new wardrobe and I hoped she might meet me some acceptable gentleman and regain her confidence. After all she was only forty-three years old. Sam was incandescent with rage and disapproved of me sending her on holi-day but I shrugged him off; he was of no consequence and we would soon be rid of him, or so I thought.

Graham, Effie, the children and I took her to the dock to see her off and she was in good form as we waved her goodbye, to be welcomed back a month later having visited exotic places such as Tonga and Samoa. Sam stayed in her house to protect it from being burgled but I knew that he was rifling through her things and I told him not to. When she returned she had a certain strange arrogance about her. During our first conversation she stated that it was only right that I pay for her holidays now as when I was a child I had cost her a fortune. I was slightly taken aback but I overlooked it.

I had modelling jobs, television commercials and would make up the money in no time.

Adam was still on crutches at Stefan's funeral but after ten months of following the doctor's advice and never once using that leg, the bone had miraculously regrown smoothly and at our final appointment the doctor told him, 'You are cured; you can walk without your crutches now.' But he had got so used to galloping around and swinging himself on two solid sticks, that he was unable to move without them. There followed a sweet incident outside in the doctor's waiting room when two elderly ladies became very tearful whilst watching him attempt to walk to the doctor's encouraging words: 'Put down your crutches and walk, you are healed!' he said. An almost Biblical scene. In the end it was easier to keep the crutches for the meantime and Adam galloped on them happily until we gradually weaned him off. It only took a couple of weeks to retrain him.

One hot day when I was alone in the house and the air was still and silent with even the birds having taken cover, I heard a terrible noise in the back garden. On investigation, I witnessed the most horrid spectacle of a huge wasp and a tarantula having a fight. The hornet wasp was dragging the great spider along the path and I watched with awe at the wasp's success. I learnt later that this is the way this particular breed of Australian hornet survives. They sting the tarantula with a paralysing toxin and then drag and conceal it in some shady spot before laying their eggs in the spider's cavity. When the young are born they feed on the still-alive spider, eating it from the inside out. Nature is brutal and savage down under; I had to get away from this dreadful place.

Stefan was gone, my son was restored to health, my career was going well and all my thoughts revolved around London. Then came the day when I asked my mother, 'When shall we go home?' But she said she wasn't ready and that she liked her garden and didn't want to leave it yet, which I thought was odd. I suspected that maybe she had a lover who she wasn't telling me about. 'I have stayed here this long because of you,' I told her with deadly calmness, 'I stayed out of my responsibility to you and I haven't had a single happy day here.' I remember that we were driving in the car, with her in the back seat and I started to find her attitude very annoying. 'Mum! I have always hated it here, I don't want to die here, I must go home, I must go to Harrods, I want to see my dad, who has never met my children, I miss my friends. I am going home and I'm going to marry an Englishman of distinction and consequence and live in Knightsbridge, as near as possible to Sloane Square, and forget about my seven years on Devil's Island. I'm bloody well going home.'

There was a short silence and then all of a sudden she said with clear venom, 'That means you don't love me at all.' I was so taken aback by her total lack of interest in my feelings and happiness that I burst out laughing. I laughed and laughed as I drove and she remained silent. I think she preferred not speaking to me rather apologising for her bad behaviour over the years. I had done all in my power to be the best of daughters; I had been a good person to the wrong people and had nothing on my conscience, so I decided to leave her. Bloody well stay here then, I thought. Drink yourself to death like all the others. I shall not stay here and rot and waste my life; I am going home.

I don't do 'victim', I shall do victory.

Chapter 10

My mother barely spoke to me for the next few weeks and Graham watched me suspiciously, thoroughly unnerved that I was now appearing daily on television commercials. As always he would snap, 'We're not put on this earth to enjoy ourselves you know,' but that phrase had ceased to bother me by now and I laughed in his face. I was totally unaffected by anything he said. We still slept in the same bed but we went to bed at different times. He would drunkenly turn in early while I sat up and read my book and then I used to tiptoe down the corridor to hear if he was snoring and it was safe to quietly slip into my side of the bed. His hatred of me grew but he spent a great deal of time at my mother's house and I was very pleased to have the time on my own. One weekend Graham and three friends went off on a fishing trip. I was thrilled to have the house to myself and on the Saturday evening, when the children were asleep, I opened a bottle of red wine, sat at the dining room table and wrote letters to my friends in England. The next day I was full of energy so I thought I would clean the house. I vigorously scrubbed the bathroom and in the afternoon I drove to explore a newly opened shopping centre which was fifteen miles away.

Graham came home on Sunday night and by Monday night he was storming around the house in a rage but refusing to tell me why, not that I particularly cared. Eventually he started to rant that he knew exactly what I had been up to all weekend. Having found the empty wine bottle in the rubbish, he had come to the conclusion that I had had a man staying over. I looked back at him blankly as Graham told me that it had definitely been a tall man, because when having a shower he'd noticed that the water jet, which normally fell on the back of his neck, had on this occasion sprayed high over his head. Therefore, this man had had a shower in the morning and moved the attachment to suit his height. Subsequently I had driven him home, according to Graham, because he had checked the mileage and the petrol.

In all my years in Australia I never once (apart from dear Professor Leeton) met a man that I would have considered as a love interest. I was certainly not going to exchange one Australian for another Australian. I don't think Graham truly loved me at all; I was his wife and he felt a possessive spite that drove him to make sure I wasn't enjoying myself too much. He had such a sense of superiority that he felt it entitled him to be a bully and put his needs and controlling opinions above all others. For our entire married life he had maintained a total disregard for my feelings and fears. I had observed him for long enough to note that in order for him to feel really good, he would need to belittle and criticise me constantly. He revelled in seeing me unhappy, desperately struggling to control my mother, run the household without a cleaner, be a good mum and work to pay the bills all at the same time. That summer he also developed a liking for nude sunbathing and each Saturday and Sunday, after a few drinks, he would lie in the garden stark naked. As I looked out of the kitchen window it appeared as though there was a dead body lying there. A couple of times a girlfriend popped over with her children and I was ashamed, especially when the little children giggled.

That year I spent my last Christmas at Effie's house. I knew I could never endure the ghastly tradition again. Ian was there with his wife Sandra; I hadn't seen them for two years but we did not speak as I still hadn't forgiven him about that lovely dog. He had grown rather corpulent and red-faced due to his drinking habits and his eyes were bloodshot. Graham was not speaking to him either, except to say that his eyes looked like 'piss holes in the snow' and later call him 'pus eyes'. They had had a disagreement at work after Graham lost his driving licence; he'd had to stay in the office and swap jobs with Ian, who was now on the road and bore a grudge because he didn't like it. We all posed for a group photograph, but we hardly spoke.

Graham always pleaded poverty and business problems to explain why I had to buy all the children's clothes and even when it was my own money he said it was ridiculous for me to waste it on leather shoes because they would soon grow out of them. I should buy plastic ones instead.

My agent, Laurie Bourne, had hired a big garden in a lovely venue one Saturday afternoon in order to give a Christmas party for all the models on his books and also his favourite clients. I had been looking forward to it and dressed in white broderie anglaise with a flouncy skirt and matching top exposing a bit of tanned midriff. Around my waist I tied a bright pink-patterned sash with fringing and the outfit looked good. When it came time to leave for the party my car keys were nowhere to be found, so I started a frantic search while Graham looked on pleading innocence. Although beautifully dressed I remember tipping all the kitchen rubbish out and rummaging desperately. I suspected him of having hidden them and in the end I called for a taxi and got to the party late. On another occasion, I had returned from a job at 3 p.m., being in good time to pick the children up from school and kindergarten, and I was in the bedroom changing my clothes and still in full make-up, when suddenly I heard a slight movement in the hall. I was alarmed, as my area was always deathly quiet in the afternoons and I had heard no footsteps beforehand or any car driving up the gravel. The bedroom was at the front of the house and right next to the hall in question, so I rushed out half-naked in my underwear thinking I had an intruder. It was Graham; he had silently returned, possibly by taxi and tiptoed into the house. He stormed up to me and shoved me roughly out of his way as he went into the bedroom and looked under the bed. 'What the hell are you doing?' I asked incredulously but by now he was wordlessly opening the cupboards and it dawned on me that he was looking for a man. He admitted as much and shouted at me that he had been speaking to his brother and his friends who assured him that I must have somebody else. His exact words were, 'Seeing as I'm not getting any somebody else must be getting it.' Ironically he had always called me a prude because I refused to participate in the wife-swapping club and yet here he was, accusing me of precisely what he had previously wanted me to do. I was very amused, I laughed myself silly.

The smile was wiped off my face when my mother came to see me one afternoon, slightly the worse for drink. She was in my bedroom, sipping some white wine while sitting on the edge of the bed and watching me put on my make-up and we were chatting routinely. As always, I spoke of my unhappy marriage to Graham and my longing to escape. She didn't show me any sympathy whatsoever and occasionally replied that it was my duty to stay in Australia. I suspected that she wanted me to stay for her convenience and I told her that I'd already stayed far longer than I'd intended and had fulfilled my duty towards her above and beyond all expectations. I reminded her of the promise she'd made before she came to Australia, that she and I would return to London immediately after Stefan's death, and said how disappointed I was that she was showing no sign of keeping her word.

Her face took on a funny look, which I initially put down to the drink, and she said to me, 'There's something I must tell you.' I turned around to give her my full attention but then she said, 'Oh, maybe I shouldn't really tell you.' She went to and fro trying to decide whether to speak and in the end I got a bit impatient and said, 'For heaven's sake, don't give half a story. Either tell me or don't tell me!' So she told me that she and Graham were having an affair. At first I thought she was joking and was stunned into silence but then she said, 'My goodness, hasn't he got a big one,' and I realised that she was telling the truth. I listened in deadly silence.

I felt sick, as if someone had kicked me in the stomach. I suddenly thought of the Bible's sixth commandment, 'honour thy father and thy mother', and it occurred to me that there should have been one telling people to honour thy daughter. I realised that I had stupidly been entangled in a web of deceit spun by her and Graham and felt disgusted and betrayed. I didn't ask for any details but it made sense when I remembered all those evening visits that Graham used to pay my mother to cheer her up, for which I was so grateful at the time. The look on her face was so viciously vengeful that it took all my composure to restrain myself from screaming. Her expression suddenly reminded me of a snake's; cold and watchful, waiting for my reaction. With an agonising effort of self-control I somehow managed to keep my poise, though she commented that my face had been rendered pale with fury. I was incensed that during all that time I had only stayed there out of duty to her, she had been abusing my kindness and good nature. I asked her to leave, as I didn't want to talk to her anymore. My loyalty and responsibility to my mother was the one thing keeping me from leaving Australia and after this treachery I felt the link was broken and I was determined to make my escape with all haste.

I didn't challenge Graham regarding this information in the immediate aftermath, as by this time, despite living in the same house, we hadn't spoken at all for the last six months. We were total strangers, living under the same roof, sharing the same bed but barely exchanging a word. He was hostile and furious enough knowing that I had plenty of money and could leave of my own volition and telling him of my imminent departure would only have spelled more trouble, so I waited till closer to the time to break it to him. Meanwhile, I had been offered a three-month contract to appear in *The Sullivans* and play a friend of a friend who had come from England. I was tempted but I am not an actress by nature, being prone to the giggles in serious moments, and I turned it down as I was planning to leave Australia anyway the following week. Laurie Bourne told me I was completely nuts, as people were desperately lining up to get a part in this immensely popular drama.

Graham had been listening to my intention to leave for years but I don't think he actually thought I would do it. However, it came as no surprise to him when I said that the business with my mother was the last straw. We were sitting in the TV room and I was quite calm and told him simply and forcibly that I wanted 'amicable' split. I would have the children educated properly in England – I especially didn't want my daughter growing up speaking with an Australian accent – and would send them to him every holiday. He agreed and we had a reasonable conversation, even discussing how to come to an arrangement for enjoying alternate Christmases with the children. He readily agreed to everything, not even grumbling about paying me for my half-share of the house, which he wanted to retain. I was pleased with him keeping the house, as it would give the children stability and continuity. Bizarrely, whilst we were talking about the children, he made his one and only demand, which was for him to be allowed to keep a painting which I had brought over from England and was quite valuable; an English countryside scene by an artist called Walter Williams that hung above the mantelpiece in the sitting room. It had been given to me many years ago by Count Zdzislaw Zamoyski, whose mother had known my grandfather, and Graham was extremely keen that it remain with him. His concern for his children's welfare clearly couldn't compete with his greed to keep what was an ordinary, if beautiful, painting. He told me that he was not suited for marriage and fatherhood and preferred 'baching it', meaning life as a bachelor was more to his liking. He could now pursue his amusements of drinking to excess and visiting massage parlours without hindrance. We spent a calm evening discussing the advantage of such an arrangement and with this heartening thought I went to bed confident and in some peace of mind.

The next evening, when he returned from the city he announced that he had spoken to his brother and some friends who had advised him 'not to let the bitch get away with it'. He would feel foolish if I was to remove the children and people would think he was odd and his reputation would plummet. He was fond of them, of course, but I felt he wanted to keep them for appearance's sake and that that was why he was now so adamant that he would sue me for full custody. Sam, the troublemaker, happened to be in my house that evening. He had called in uninvited and stayed observing and relishing the drama. I resented his presence and wanted him gone but Sam was never one easy to get rid of; he just hung around, no matter how many hints were dropped. I was stricken with terror at what Graham had just said. I implored him to be merciful. I screamed and clutched and begged him but it was no good. I remember I was holding a mug of tea and in a moment of desperation hurled it across the room, splashing the walls and even the ceiling. I was hysterical with all the ferocity of devoted motherhood; I was like an animal savagely fighting for my young. Then Sam said to Graham, 'Shall I hold her down?' and they moved towards me, intending to wrestle me to the ground. I took the car keys and I drove wildly to my friend Sue's house and pounded on her door but she was out and her mother was there babysitting instead. The mother gave me no comfort and only reminded me that Adam and Camilla were Graham's children too. 'But he's an irresponsible drunk,' I wailed. 'He does nothing for their welfare, sleeps all weekend long and staggers around the house after too much brandy on Saturdays.' I drove home and when I got there Sam had left to go to my mother's while Graham had passed out drunkenly on the sofa and I noticed a cigarette burn on the furniture. The next day, my little son went into the TV room and asked, 'What's happened here?' looking at the tea stains on the wall and on the ceiling and the upturned furniture. I replied, 'Mummy spilt her tea,' and he looked at me mystified.

Mother Anguish

I went to the Qantas office in the city and booked a ticket for me and the children for as soon as possible. I gave instructions that if anyone was to enquire about my name with the airline, no information was to be given. Qantas did two routes between Melbourne and Heathrow; one went Melbourne, Perth, Bombay, Heathrow and the other Melbourne, Sydney, Singapore, Heathrow. The route via Perth was faster but it meant that the plane would still be over Australian territory for five hours and I couldn't take that risk in case Graham tried to stop me. Sydney was an hour's flight from Melbourne and then it would be out of Australian airspace. The flight was leaving at 11 a.m. and the day before I packed and hid my suitcase in the garage. Graham was still forbidden to drive but I decided not to take the car to the airport because I didn't want to alert him to the fact that I had done a runner before I was safely on English soil. The morning of my escape I woke early and I lay there blinking and thinking what a momentous day this would be in my life.

The previous night, Graham had had too much to drink and to my dismay he awoke with a hangover and declared that he might not go to work that day. 'Don't be silly,' I said, 'why don't you just go and you can always get a taxi home later if you don't feel well.' I was much relieved when he left. I threw myself into a frenzy of preparation for departure. I stole Graham's passport so that he could not follow me, I rang the school to say that Adam had a bug and would not be coming in that day and I wrote Graham a note, which I left on the kitchen shelf, saying that I was going away for the weekend. I said nothing of my plans to my mother and did not bid her goodbye as I could not trust her at all now. I hugged my dogs Gabby, Mishy and Mosky goodbye and they all looked at me knowingly. I filled their water bowl and left my house with one last slightly sentimental look around the sitting room, saying farewell to all my possessions. I departed with a suitcase and a child under each arm. I had no compunction about taking the children away from Graham; he was not a responsible or attentive father. He was drunk all weekend long when he should have been playing daddy and he hardly saw them in the week, as by the time he used to return home from the city they were already asleep. He had refused us central heating and air conditioning for no reason whatsoever, as he had enough money for drinking and visiting hookers. If he could afford that then he could have afforded to have kept his children warm.

At the airport I was told all the planes were grounded because of the fog. 'What fog?' I said, with a hint of panic in my voice. It was a beautiful, sunny January day; high summer and not a cloud in the sky. 'There is fog in Sydney,' I was told and as that was to be our first stop, nothing could land until it had lifted. I had a very anxious two-hour wait as the departure lounge filled up with people sitting on the floor. But then suddenly it was announced that my flight was boarding. I cannot put it into words my feeling of exultation when I heard the aeroplane engines rev and we took off.

I was going home! Home to England and my beloved London town. I would forget all about the nightmare that had been Australia; I would put all those memories of blackness and doom behind me and start afresh. I was still young.

During my flight I was so excited that I couldn't help telling my story to a steward. He was aghast that I was on the run and wished me luck. Looking out of the window as the plane flew over England my eyes welled up. At Heathrow I took a taxi. Oh, the bliss of sitting in a taxi, driving through London and seeing familiar streets. I thanked God for my deliverance from hell.

I had informed my old friends that I was coming and Olga said that the children and I could stay with her. I was desperate to settle down quickly and find an Englishman who could look after and protect me because I was sure that Graham would follow. Despite Olga's previous hurtful betrayal, she appeared willing to make amends and I knew I could count on her to always be

Mother Anguish

surrounded by men. Olga lived in Kensington Church Street and seemed delighted to see me. She adored my little children and immediately invited some friends over that evening. How vibrant London people were compared to Australians; I was in heaven.

On my return to England it was all made clear as to who was and was not on my side. I telephoned my mother, almost as an exercise to see what reaction I would get when she found out that I was in London. I had money but I thought to put her to the test just for fun. I would ask for a small donation whilst I was sorting out my bank transfers and things; just a bit to tide me over for a short while. She told me I was no child of hers and that she would not give me a penny. 'Not a penny, not a penny,' she kept repeating and I could hear Sam egging her on in the background. But by this time I was past caring as I thought I had done my duty by her and been the best of daughters. I also telephoned my friend Sue in Melbourne and she asked me to ring Graham as he was busily seeking legal advice. So I called Graham and whilst he was shouting and threatening me, saying he was going to make me sorry I was born, I very calmly told him, 'You have underestimated me.' Later on in court it was to be read out in his statement that I had said 'I have outsmarted you' but that was incorrect.

I then spoke to my dad, who I had not seen for so very long. He was overjoyed to hear from me and we met up the next day. He was unhappily married to a woman with a gambling habit and I resolved to be a wonderful daughter to him and cheer him up as much as I could. From then on we would meet often and I was thrilled to be have him back in my life.

Two days later Olga had a gentleman caller whom she explained she had met in a club. She asked me to let him in and keep him chatting until she was ready as she hadn't finished her make-up. She told me that he was 'very beefy'. I opened the door to a dangerous-looking man leaning against the door frame. He was large and menacing and dressed like a spiv. He was wearing jeans, cowboy boots, a brown bomber jacket and a half-undone shirt that exposed his chest hair, amongst which nestled a large scorpion medallion. He said his name was Dick and I detected a strong cockney accent. We sat down and he told me he had been a nightclub bouncer. I listened agog to his tales of how to control fights; if ever the need should arise in a bar for one to fend for oneself with a broken glass or bottle, one was not to smash it on the bar in a downward motion and lift it back up to warn the opponent (or worse). One must always smash the glass in an upward motion and keep going straight for the enemy's face in a single sweep, thereby not wasting time. Golly, I thought, this is what I need to frighten Graham off in case he comes after me. Dick was twelve years older than me and had been divorced for five years but tall and quite handsome and I wondered what he would look like dressed in a proper suit and wearing a tie. And, indeed, this alarming and intimidating man was to become my second husband. We spent twenty minutes chatting and I thought he had an offbeat sense of humour. I told him I had just arrived in London, having run away from my husband and he frowned heavily, perhaps contemplating the inescapable fact that trouble would follow. Trouble obviously appealed to him, as he invited me for lunch at his place on the following Sunday; he said he was having a couple of friends round so I accepted.

His flat was a basement in Paddington. I descended the steps with a psychic feeling that this would be a significant day in my life, though I didn't much care for basements with heaps of smelly dustbins at the front. I carefully lifted my best coat at the back to stop it being soiled while walking down the wet stairs. I had dressed that day in my best cream jeans and peach silk shirt. His flat was unlike anything I had ever seen before. It had no windows and there was a musty smell. The walls were covered in red flock wallpaper and the floor was strewn with natural-shaped sheepskin rugs that looked like road kill. I was amused when passing by his bedroom to see the bed covered in an acrylic tiger-skin cover.

Mother Anguish

His friends were pleasant enough though frightfully common. One girl there was an ex-girlfriend of Dick's. She was blonde, flirtatious and curvaceous and disliked me on sight, commenting on the fact that I was Polish with a slight barb and sneer which I graciously accepted with a superior half-smile and a shrug. I noticed that Dick drank very heavily, Canadian Club whisky with ginger ale, but he was a cheerful drunk and later in the day he asked me to come to the pub with him. He said he went to the Archery Tavern in Bayswater every evening and played darts. There I met his other male friends, a jovial bunch of small-time crooks, builders like himself, plumbers and 'sparks', meaning electricians. I found their humour infinitely entertaining but very coarse. I had never been in such company before; I had mixed with the lower middle class in Australia but this was something else. They were full of loud banter and on learning that my name was Basia, they all hooted with laughter that, although this was our first date, if we ended up getting married I would be 'Basher Briggs'. He drove me home, stopping at his favourite fish-and-chip shop for some cod and chips wrapped in newspaper.

In conversation with Dick, however drunk he was, I detected a sharp mathematical brain and decided that he could be more successful in his trade if he mixed with better company. He just needed a few introductions to my rich friends to get decent contracts for work and then surely he could become a master builder or property developer with the right guidance. I decided he needed mothering and advancing into better spheres of society. He in turn asked me to move in with him, so that when Graham came looking for me he could 'see him off' and I agreed as I required a villain. We had only known each other for three days but I was in desperate need of a protector. Marriage appeared out of the question at the time because we were of such different backgrounds and he spoke with a cockney accent. It's not that I fancied 'a bit of rough'; I just needed a bit of security. He was strong and savage, all a man should be, and to show my gratitude for his help, I would make him prosperous.

Although I had stolen Graham's passport and it amused me to imagine him tearing the house apart searching for it, he succeeded in obtaining a replacement passport within three weeks. He also instructed lawyers to sue me for full custody and papers were served personally to my father's address. I ended up in the High Court of England on a charge of kidnapping and stood in the witness box like a common criminal. Despite the charges against me being dropped, the law stated that irrespective of the physical violence and abuse I had suffered and Graham's rampant adultery, my children still came under the jurisdiction of the Australian courts, as they were born of an Australian father on Australian soil. So Graham took them back to Melbourne and a vicious, expensive legal standoff followed, during which the children flew back and forth and I flew back and forth and it seemed we spent all of their childhood crying at airports. Despite my escape from the hell I had endured in Australia, these partings were to be amongst the worst times of my life.

During the early days with Dick I was beset by such problems that it almost became a comedy. I had intended upon leaving Graham to 'make an impressive marriage' and in many ways I did. At the time we both felt that we were above each other: Dick looked down at me for being Polish and I looked down at him for being a small-time, drunken cockney builder who lived in a Paddington basement; but I was on a mission to change everything about him, from the way he dressed to the way he behaved and what he ate. I committed to changing the man into someone who did exactly as I pleased and he knew it was all for his good too, so didn't argue too much.

First of all I had to get rid of the red flock wallpaper on his walls and also the synthetic tiger-skin duvet cover on his bed. I went to Peter Jones and bought pure cotton bedding and chucked out his sheepskin floor mats. I placed flowerpots full of blooms by the front of the door, put up hanging baskets and encouraged the neighbours upstairs to keep their rubbish bins tidy in the cupboards provided under the pavement. It was difficult at first to change his style of clothes, as he was devoted to his bomber jackets and scorpion medallion, and absolutely impossible to get him to wear a tie; it seemed he would as soon wear one as wear a hangman's noose.

I took him to meet some friends of mine living in Richmond. Jeremy was a successful solicitor and his wife Clarissa was a beautiful housewife. They mistrusted Dick and I could see that he felt uncomfortable in their company. Afterwards, on our way home Dick referred to them scornfully as 'fat cats' and the next day Jeremy tactfully described Dick as 'a rough diamond'. We never socialised with them again but I think Dick noted their lovely house and felt envy and desire for their gracious lifestyle. Bomber jackets on grown men of over thirty and elegance don't go together and gradually he allowed me to choose his shirts. It will only be a matter of time before he wears a tie, I thought.

Dick first proposed to me when we were in a taxi en route to a rock concert in Camden. However, he had had rather too much to drink and on stepping out of the cab, he fell over with his arm around me, so we both went crashing to the ground together. I was very cross and told him to ask me again when he was sober. The manager of The Victoria pub in Strathearn Place insisted on giving us a reception as a wedding present. I would have preferred Claridges but gave in on this occasion.

I divorced Graham on the grounds of adultery; committed with someone called Bronwen, who agreed to be named as she wanted to marry Graham. I was told by Effie that this Bronwen had had blows with my mother when she heard of the concurrent affair. I married Dick as soon as my divorce from Graham was finalised. I was desperate for custody of Adam and Camilla and thought that to this end, being a stable married woman would be preferable to being a single mum.

My children were with me in London at the time and I enjoyed dressing them up for my wedding. My little daughter Camilla wore white lace and little white socks and they both looked a picture. I didn't have a proper bridesmaid as, not wanting me to marry Dick, most of my friends had refused to attend, so she took the role instead. Dick on the other hand had two 'best men', both unsavoury types and they turned up dreadfully inebriated. Dick didn't own a suit, so on the day he wore a blazer and slacks (and a tie). It was a strange event which I approached with a bit of trepidation and I was upset for my father who had for days tried to talk me out of it, saying, 'You are both moulded from different clay.' When that didn't work he had said, 'How can you lower yourself so?' My father had wanted me to marry someone respectable but, as before, I had felt headstrong. He was stony-faced in the company of Dick's rowdy, drunken friends, mostly East End hoodlums in dark glasses, and didn't stay for the reception. My best girlfriend too voiced her opinion and was unspeakably beastly to me, telling me, 'You won't be able to bring yourself down to his level and he is not capable of rising to yours.'

Regardless of his disappointment in my choice of husband, I am so pleased I had the chance to get to know my father upon my return to London, as he died the following year of a heart attack. I always thought he was the healthiest man in London; he didn't drink or smoke, he played tennis and went skiing in Austria at every opportunity. When in England, at the slightest flurry of snow he would grab his skis and dash to Hampstead Heath, where he said one could enjoy perfectly good cross-country skiing. He seemed in robust health and often used to joke that he would live to the age of 109. It is a tragic fact of life that the first sign of heart disease is often sudden death.

The day he died his wife telephoned me in the morning as I lay sleeping. 'Your father is dead,' she wailed hysterically. I held my forehead and said, 'What are you saying? What are you saying?' but received no sensible answer so I hurriedly dressed and ran into the road to catch a taxi to Courtfield Gardens where he lived. An ambulance was standing outside the house and I rushed up the stairs to his flat. He lay in bed on his back, fully covered by his bed-clothes and looking dignified despite his jaw having slackened. His wife had informed a couple of neighbours who came in to see the body and one of them had called the priest, which was a nice Polish ritual. We all stood around my father's bed saying prayers and holding lit candles. Then the doctor came and pronounced that it had most likely been a heart attack. He was very kind and sat for a while with me as my father's wife went to pick up her children from school. Soon he was gone too though and I was left all alone with my dead father while I waited for the wife to come back. Utterly bewildered, I gazed at length at his lifeless face and kept saying, 'What the hell happened to you?' I had an overwhelming need to tell somebody what had happened but everyone was out and so I was forced to give up.

The ambulance men came to remove his body and I respectfully left the room as I didn't want to see him naked. Then they emerged with my father in a black body bag, strapped to a stretcher with parcel tape. They carried him out of his bedroom vertically to get him through the door and I wept at the sight. I felt so heartbroken at his death. When I had escaped from Melbourne he had been so happy and welcoming. He was understanding when I told him of my unhappy marriage, whereas others had been judgemental. I'll never forget the experience of visiting his ancestral home in Poland some years later and seeing the splendour from whence he came; it really was unreservedly magnificent and ever since I've felt guilty for my previous feelings of shame towards my Polish roots and for doing disservice to his family's good name. Soon afterwards I went to the coroner's court to observe the formalities. A jolly, rotund red-faced coroner informed me that it had been a massive coronary clot; 'absolutely massive', he repeated a couple of times, as if it were a compliment. Then I went to Kenyon's Undertakers in Marloes Road and made the necessary arrangements. When the undertaker had left the room momentarily, I sneaked a look at the big book wherein he had written my father's details. Next to his name I saw he had written 'Good week!' Presumably business was brisk and one family's tragedy is another's profit. It was the end of October by the time I went to register his death at the side entrance of Chelsea Town Hall; I gave all his details and then emerged into the King's Road on a dark and rainy early evening.

There were many awful times at the beginning of my marriage to Dick; although he was cheerful and full of fun whilst sober in the daytime, he nevertheless was a troublesome and alarming drunk and whenever my children were with me in London, he would frighten them after being in the pub all evening. After just a short while under the same roof they had bitten their nails to the quick with fear. He was simply too dangerous and irresponsible to be around my son and daughter. When Adam was just five or six, he decided to teach him how to throw a knife, using a nearby tree for target practice. Little Adam, incapable of emulating Dick's deadly aim, missed to the right of the tree and the blade whistled just past the head of a nearby pedestrian. Whilst I was doing my utmost to change Dick's ways and sober him up, I voluntarily let my children spend some time in Australia for their own mental wellbeing and Graham and I signed an agreement. The alternative would have been to follow the English tradition of placing them in boarding schools to be cared for by total strangers, which I didn't want to inflict upon them at such an early age, having myself been institutionalised far too young. At least in Australia they had family support close by, no matter how ghastly. But I was beyond desolate when separated from the kids and at night when Dick was sleeping I used to sit on the bathroom floor and weep hysterically for hours. After things had calmed down somewhat with Dick, they resumed their regular visits from Australia and always stayed for two months in their summer holidays.

From the off, my friends didn't like Dick at all and were horrified by our marriage but they were too scared to say so in his company as his temper was by his own admission 'volatile'. One well-known estate agent in Bayswater made that mistake outside The Victoria and Dick picked him up, punched him and hurled him through the air so that he landed on the other side of the pavement in the gutter. I detected, however, that under that rough and terrifying exterior was a man with the raw materials to make something of himself. He was so clever mathematically but mixed with ghastly riff-raff; mostly loud drunks who boasted that they had been in the SAS, which I am sure was a load of codswallop. I had to freeze out these unsuitable ruffians and change Dick's habits, as he spent every single evening in the pub playing darts and went twice on Saturdays and Sundays, thereby drinking far too much Canadian Club whisky, not to mention the wine he had at lunchtime on the weekends. I gradually persuaded Dick that there were other, more rewarding, ways to spend one's time than going to the pub each day and I arranged to go to the opera or the theatre and then gave him books to read. In no time at all he was hooked on the writings of Somerset Maugham and I knew I was halfway there. Changing his eating habits wasn't easy either, as he loved his fried white bread and full English breakfasts. He point-blank refused to be a vegetarian like me, maintaining that he 'wasn't a rabbit' but gradually I introduced brown bread, salads and broccoli and in time he grew to prefer it.

I was resolutely cheerful and hopeful, though there were times when my faith wavered. Once, we experienced a dodgy evening out at dinner with friends of mine who were in the music business. About ten of us had gone to a restaurant in Kensington and I was seated on one side of a long, narrow table next to a musician from a very famous band, still well known today. Dick was seated opposite and halfway through the meal he decided that the musician was being a bit too tactile with me. Suddenly Dick reached out a great arm, grabbed this guy by the hair, lifted him up over the table and smashed him in the face, knocking him out totally. I gasped as I saw the man's nose bleeding and his eye swelling and needless to say we both left. I told Dick I could handle men in my own way in future but even so, it was a good lesson to anyone else who was tempted to take liberties with my person and part of me was sort of pleased.

I had suffered such immense emotional strain being married to a heavy drinker like Graham for all those years and it had worn away my nerves. I nagged, cried and cajoled, pleading for Dick to stop drinking; it wasn't easy but in 1989 he stopped completely both for my sake and that of his health. He concentrated instead on the good things in life such as making his Hyde Park improvements, for which he was eventually to receive an OBE (An award he nicknamed 'Our Basia's Efforts'). He started to wear corduroy trousers, Barbour jackets and tweed caps, looking in no time like an English squire. These days Dick's usual attire is a three-piece, pinstripe suit from Savile Row with a white stiff-collared shirt and gentleman's brogues.

Despite his transformation, it was still a foolhardy man who thought he could get away with any violence when Dick was around, as a couple of bank robbers were to find out. I think being a street fighter is in Dick's DNA, as one sunny day in 1988 when he was walking up Bishop's Bridge Road, he heard a dreadful commotion coming from a hold-up inside a Williams and Glyn bank and so, being Dick, he relished the idea of challenging singlehandedly the two bank robbers, armed with a hammer and a gun, that he found within. Anything for a good fight. The incident was reported in the newspapers as one of the bank's customers was a journalist for the *Evening Standard*. The journalist's child was urinating in fright while they and all the other terrified clients were made to lie on the floor. Everyone was screaming while one robber was on the counter trying to smash the window, yelling, 'Money, money!' At this point Dick apparently burst in like a 'Human Bullet', a moniker that made the headline of the article. He was like a forward in a rugby scrum as he jumped on to the two men and they got to painfully and humiliatingly experience his considerable ability at martial arts. When Dick thought he was going to be shot, he crouched to the ground and the robber behind him hit him hard on the head with a hammer. Then, adrenaline fuelled, Dick chased them out of the bank and rescued the hostages, the bank staff having fled. Extraordinary.

Dick was much praised to the press by Detective Sergeant David Gaywood at Paddington Green Police Station, who said, 'What he did was extremely brave; to take on one man with a large hammer and another with a gun. No doubt but for his action they would have been able to escape with a considerable amount of money, or someone may have been killed.' My favourite quote, though, came from a Mr Bert Gibbs who was painting the bank manager's office and saw what was happening. He told the paper that he had picked up a hammer and was going to 'have a go' but couldn't get through the door as he had taken the handles off. I have the newspaper cutting laminated to this day and displayed on the guest bathroom wall.

I was at home quietly sunbathing and minding my own business that day when I saw Dick arrive, grinning broadly and covered in blood, as head wounds tend to gush alarmingly. To my exasperation he refused to go to hospital, telling me not to make a fuss, and insisted on going to the pub instead as he said he needed a stiff drink. He needed strong painkillers that night too. The next day his wound had spread wide open and had a curly look around the edges, so he sought medical attention and was reprimanded at the hospital since by then it was difficult to stitch up. He was still in some pain but very cheerful about his adventure. Afterwards he was obliged to give a statement to the police and in due course the bank offered him a reward of £500 to be given to his favourite charity, so he donated it to the widows of the soldiers killed in the Hyde Park bombing.

The 1980s was a boom time in London property and many of my friends recommended Dick for work. In no time at all he had a large company and a number of staff. One of my friends, John Chudzynski, was an architectural surveyor and he threw masses of jobs our way, helping along Dick's swift ascendancy to becoming a successful property developer.

William Worsley, son of the Lord Lieutenant of Yorkshire, found a fabulously large but totally dilapidated maisonette in Sloane Gardens and wondered if he and Dick should do it up as a development and sell it. But as soon as I saw it I fell in love and decided I must have it for myself. It really was a ruin, with broken windows and pigeon droppings throughout, but we bought it regardless, using the profits from Dick's burgeoning business and a portion of the inheritance my recently deceased grandfather had left me. It was as though this house had been standing there waiting for me all its life, and all roads had led me to it. And indeed I live here and always will. I have the store Peter Jones just outside at the front and a garden with nesting robins at the back and I can walk to Harrods. Utter bliss; I was back where I belonged. Whenever I now see William, we always joke about it and I always give him a kiss and say, 'Thank you for finding me a home!'

This is the area I knew as a child and I find memories of my mother in her youth and others I have loved on every corner.

Chapter 11

Long before our move to Sloane Gardens, after some two years back in London, I had visited Melbourne for just a couple of weeks as it was my son's birthday. I kept patting my return ticket in my pocket but the memories made me feel ill and uneasy. Whenever I went back there to visit the children I always felt like the Count of Monte Cristo returning to the Château d'If. I stayed at an American-style motel, nearby my old house where the children lived. The rooms at the motel had doors which were accessible from the street and there was no security. One night, soon after my arrival, Graham came knocking, having asked at the reception which number room I was staying in. He insisted that I let him in so he could 'just sit on the end of your bed and have a chat' but I told him to go away with imperious disregard. He became abusive and swore, just like old times, calling me a 'stuck-up bitch'. He knocked and pounded at the door while my nerves jangled and I threatened him with calling the police. Eventually he left and I slept fitfully and fretfully, dozing off and then waking in a sweat having imagined him gaining entry into my room. The next day I asked the reception to change my room, explaining what had happened and they promised to never give out any information again.

As if that wasn't enough trouble, my son had a birthday party the following night with a bonfire and fireworks. The next day he and a few of his little friends were playing in the remaining ashes and raking them about, when Adam had the bright idea of getting some petrol from the garage to liven up the still-glowing embers. He poured the petrol on and half-blew himself up, receiving terrible first- and second-degree burns to his whole arm and down one side of his body. I rushed to get him medical attention and he recovered but it was a salutary lesson not to play with fire. He spent some time with bandages covering his first-degree burns and developed blisters the size of golf balls elsewhere.

Having tended to Adam's injuries and ensured that he was on the road to recovery, I came back to London with the arrangement that the children would be sent to me in two months' time. I found these separations heartrendingly painful, especially around teatime, bath time and bedtime; usually the busiest and jolliest times of day. I used to sit and cry pitifully for hours.

Whilst Graham had both children to look after, he wasted no time in acquiring a succession of nannies. He boasted to our friends, who then told me, that when interviewing prospective candidates in the evening, he would light the sitting room fire, give them wine and play on their sympathy. I was informed he had managed to seduce seven applicants in a row on successive nights. Eventually a kind-hearted middle-aged nun from a convent in Adelaide applied for the job. She had questioned the Catholic faith and decided she did not have a true vocation. Her name was Celeste Fogarty and she moved into the house full-time and was very dedicated and warm and the children loved her very much. She wrote me reassuring letters telling me that, for the short time that she was to be in charge of them, she would look after them carefully. I had much to be grateful to her for but perversely Graham managed to seduce her too and the poor woman had a complete nervous breakdown and left. She returned to the convent and we always exchanged Christmas cards. The children loved her until adulthood and were very upset when she died in 2010.

During this period my mother stayed in Melbourne and was sober. I telephoned the children twice a week and whenever I spoke to them, they always said her fridge was filled with delicious food and salami and whatever they wanted. My mother used to sometimes pick them up from school and care for them until

Mother Anguish

Graham came to get them after work, although she complained that he was often very late and drunk. Failing that, Effie would pick them up, so I knew they were safe with their two grannies. But still I pined and howled like an animal every time I heard their sweet little voices on the phone and consulted my lawyer constantly in order to get them back permanently, as they missed me as much as I missed them. My friend Sue often went to check in on them and whenever we spoke on the phone she would warn me that my mother and Graham were together doing their best to blacken my character and poison my children's minds against me.

The whole point of me leaving was for them to have a better life and I never meant to hurt them but as with all children of a fractured family they endured the fallout, bitterness and insecurity that are its consequences and the mental scars remain. As spiteful and antagonistic as Graham always was to me, I never expected him to create such havoc as he did in the bitter years that followed my departure. My whole existence as a mother was on the line and I would not let myself be a lifetime prisoner to his whims. I was involved with the passion of life, the passion for freedom and victory over my detractors. These confrontations were psychologically terrible for me and the children but Graham revelled in them and gloated at my unhappiness and angst.

He even joined an organisation called Parents Without Partners; he told my friend Sue that this was a splendid way for him to meet desperate women and that he had great success with the ladies. Somehow he was voted 'Single Father of the Year'. I wanted to puke when I heard this, especially as I discovered that after putting the children to bed he would frequently go out and stay away until dawn with some woman, leaving the children totally without a babysitter. I contacted my solicitor and Graham was warned never to leave the children all alone at night.

I succeeded eventually in gaining full custody of Camilla and she was educated in a traditional school in South Kensington whilst my son flew back and forth. Then my son came back to England to live full-time. I think all the travelling in his childhood imprinted itself on his mind, as now he tours the world and spends much time living in India. He often returns to London to do the season, attending Royal Ascot and Henley, and then puts on his scruffy clothes and goes back off to India. He has a liking for rough travelling in far-flung exotic places. And why not.

After two years of correspondence with my mother, throughout which she complained bitterly about Melbourne and how treacherous Graham was and how bitterly she regretted allowing Sam to inveigle himself into our lives, she eventually did come to London and a bought a house in Ealing. I don't know exactly when or how her affair with Graham ended but she gave me reason to believe that his other sexual relationships played their part. I do know that it continued for some time after I left for London, as my little son later mentioned to me that when he spent the night at her house he found it confusing to see his father emerging out of my mother's bedroom in the morning. Though my love had gone, I still felt a daughter's duty towards my mother. I continued to spend much time soul-searching; remembering her kindness to me as a child and contemplating the dramatic change in her personality that had taken place in Melbourne.

She had specifically wanted a small house so that there would be a no room for Sam but shortly afterwards Sam followed anyway and we could not dislodge him. He would live with her rent-free during the summer months, returning to Australia in the winter to enjoy the sun there. My mother once rang me in tears to say that Sam was selling off her antiques to fund his lifestyle and I rang the dealer insisting he return all her goods. I even rang the police but the items had already been sold on. I particularly missed a beautiful ormolu clock with little cherubs; I had always loved it and bloody Sam had sold it. Throughout the years he developed such a malignant hold over my mother. When I went to visit her he would often turn on the lawnmower to drown out our conversation and when she and I were sat talking in the kitchen he would stand leaning his back against the sink with an eager grin and his arms folded waiting for me to leave. Once he had settled in and his grip on her had tightened, she started to ask me for money, usually about £200 at a time. She also began to make snide comments whenever I wore something pretty. Once she noticed I had a new handbag and seemed so taken by it that I thought it would be easiest to just give it to her as a present, although I liked it very much myself. The next time I saw her she had stuffed it so full of junk and possessions that the clip had given way and it was bursting at the seams as she wrestled with it. I gulped and said nothing but then she started complaining about what a rubbishy, cheap bag I had given her. I like to think I did all I could to sober her up before she lost control again under the influence of Sam and I occasionally invited her to Sunday lunch at Pontevecchio in Old Brompton Road. She always took money from me to pay for her taxi home and it saddened me.

My mother started to drink heavily again and this time she really did lose her looks totally. I had to have her admitted to a drying-out clinic in Ealing Hospital. One day when I visited her, Sam was standing by the side of her bed smirking and I flew at him in a rage, jabbing at him with my car keys and telling him to leave us alone and get out of our lives. She was only drunk when he was there and she complained that he treated her house as his own and invited his friends. Bizarrely, when I attacked him and the nurses came running in, my mother told them to ask *me* to go. Sam sneered at me with pleasure and I cried all the way home as I knew I had lost her to this creep. In truth, however, I had lost her years ago. I attended a meeting at the hospital where a few social workers were discussing her case and we all hoped for the best but feared the worst.

I once went to her house and as she was in her sitting room, I rummaged through her bedroom cupboards, finding three bottles of whisky down amongst her shoes. One bottle was empty and two were full and I carried them to the sitting room. When she saw what I was holding she flew across the room like superwoman and tried to grab the bottles, which I refused to let go of. We stood there Velcroed and swaying before I said, 'What is more important, me or your whisky?' She answered the whisky – 'Drink is my friend,' were her exact words – so I let go and as usual returned home weeping. It was impossible to help someone who didn't want to be saved and I certainly couldn't manage it on my own.

On one occasion I telephoned her but there was no answer. I rang and rang and knew something was seriously amiss, as by then she had become a recluse and never left her home. I went to her house but she did not answer the bell or my banging on the door. I had no choice but to go to her neighbours, who were two quiet, respectable old ladies, and I asked them apologetically if I could please go through their house to the garden and climb over their back fence, which they allowed. I hung on to a drainpipe to give myself leverage and clambered over the wall. My mother's kitchen door was unlocked and as I entered the house, I felt considerable trepidation. My pulse was booming and my stomach was churning as I walked silently down the corridor to her room. She lay there in total darkness, the curtains drawn blocking out the sunny day. She was so drunk and slurring that she did not even recognise me and started speaking to me in English. I lost my temper a bit, kicking her bed frame a few times and telling her I hated her for putting me through all this. Then I made her sit up and eat a banana. I put some water by the side of her bed and left.

Another day she rang in a state of great distress to say that Sam had forced her to alter her will totally in his favour, with two of his mates acting as witnesses to it. As soon he's gone, she said, she would put it back to the way it was, in favour of my children. Alas it was not to be. She died a terrible death in 2004. I was informed by Sam that she had had a stroke, after which he had called an ambulance.

Mother Anguish

I rushed to the hospital where she lay totally unresponsive. I spoke to a doctor and was informed that in fact she hadn't had a stroke at all but had developed sepsis as a result of pneumonia. As she was not yet seventy, I thought she would rally and I sat with her all day, moistening her lips with a little sponge because her breathing was dry and rasping. I lifted her mottled hand and it dropped like a stone. I watched the monitors and talked to the doctors, who said they could do nothing to help, apart from keeping her warm, as her organs were failing. Sam and his mate from the cycling club, a witness to her will, both turned up in the afternoon and pulled up chairs to the foot of her bed and sat there cheerfully planning their upcoming cycling holiday. They chatted away merrily until I did my nut and said, 'excuse me, I am sitting at my mother's deathbed and you are being disgustingly inappropriate,' and told the nurse to order them to leave. Just before midnight, I felt the time was drawing near. I stroked her brow and held her hand and told her that she was doing very well and that she need not be frightened of what was coming. My old memories tumbled around in my brain, from the lovely woman of my childhood to the ravaged ruin that lay before me. To ease her passing I told her that she had been a very good mother and although she showed no sign of conscious-ness, I saw a large tear trickle down her cheek. It must be true what they say, that the last sensation to go is one's hearing.

The night staff, three Nigerian nurses, obviously knew when death was imminent, and they clustered silently around my mother's bed. I remember one of them leant her arms on the bed barrier and I stood on the other side. The light shone on my mother's face but otherwise the room stood in darkness and was empty. There had been two other patients in that ward earlier in the day but without me noticing they had been removed. We stood quietly and watched the monitors and every so often I looked up at the nurses who smiled kindly at me. And then she died. I could scarce believe it; she was still relatively young and I had expected her to recover and I had hoped that afterwards I would sober her up and buy her pretty dresses again. The monitor went flat and I turned to the nurses, who nodded when I asked if she was dead. I gazed up at the ceiling in case her spirit was floating and looking down on the scene and then, having made the sign of the cross, I waved her goodbye.

Meanwhile, Sam was changing the locks in my mother's house and the next day refused me entry. As she had died on the Easter bank holiday weekend, I had to wait until Tuesday to register her death. 'Present at the death', it said on the certificate and I recalled my childhood memories when it never occurred to me that my mother would ever die. I went to the undertaker to make arrangements but I was so shell-shocked at her untimely death that I did not make a fuss about the house.

The funeral took place and I did not weep. I had done all my weeping for my mother long, long ago. She was then cremated and we all repaired to a local hotel for sandwiches. Dick did not attend out of a long-lasting hatred for her but there were about twenty of us, including a friend of Sam's who I had certainly never met before and who immediately asked me if he could take and keep all my mother's flower tributes. Sam came up to me with a sly sideways look and boasted that the will was in his favour and that I was entitled to nothing.

I had notified a few of my mother's girlfriends about her death, though I did not place an obituary in the Polish paper; not because I lacked respect, but because I was aware of the many old Polish women whose chief entertainment was scouring the obituaries and turning up at funerals of strangers in the hope that they'd bump into other old Polish women and have a jolly. This peculiarity of the Polish community was made plenty evident to me in the most unpleasant way when I attended a reception at the Polish Embassy with my best friend, Daniel Topolski, a few weeks later. He had gone to get me a drink and whilst I was temporarily left standing alone, Olga's mother, the cabaret singer from all those years back, stormed up to me in a rage, demanding to know why I hadn't put my mother's obituary into the Polish newspaper. Instead of offering me kind condolences for my loss, she furiously ranted that I was a bad daughter and complained that she had been denied the pleasure of attending my mother's funeral, although the two women were not even friends, she had merely heard of my mother's death on the grapevine. She was now well over eighty years old but time had not mellowed her and she was brutal to me, which was the last thing I had expected at a party. Daniel saw this upsetting exchange and my distressed face, so he dashed across the room to my side. 'She says I have done everything wrong!' I said to him plaintively, whereupon he turned savagely to the woman and told her exactly what he thought of her with a thunderous look on his face.

All who knew Daniel remarked on his cheerfulness and charm but few apart from his Oxford Boat Race crew would have witnessed him in one of his powerful, passionate, booming rages. That passion, drive and fury made him the most successful rowing coach of all time, responsible for twelve Oxford victories. Even his children used to say he was frightening when he was angry. 'Come away from this awful woman,' he finally barked, grabbing me by the arm to lead me to safety. As we were making our exit he made one fierce final aside, speaking well within the woman's earshot: 'And if she is ever horrid to you again, I shall rip her orange wig off!' Daniel had got to know my mother very well in the preceding years and analysing both me and her was one of his amusing hobbies. He was a man of great perception and had a way of understanding humanity, always hitting the nail on the head. When he died, on 21 February 2015, I was utterly shipwrecked and did not leave the house for two weeks. This man's death completely knocked the stuffing out of me. Over the course of my life I have experienced great love and overwhelming grief.

I had in my possession all of my mother's previous wills and letters from her detailing how she had been controlled and beaten by Sam and I consulted a famous firm of solicitors which my neighbour had recommended. They charged me at a rate of £400 an hour but did little to help apart from writing endless letters to Sam, which he ignored. They put a stop on his will so that no probate could be granted and his lawyer put a stop on mine. This went on for a year whilst he lived in my mum's house and sold whatever he fancied to fund a summer holiday.

Despite spending a fortune for their services, the solicitors were unable to retrieve my mother's complete medical records from the NHS because of 'patient confidentiality'. I was very much interested to see them and find out exactly what had happened, as it was still not quite clear to me what had brought on her rapid deterioration and the discrepancy between the diagnosis of pneumonia and Sam's previous declaration of a stroke had aroused my suspicion. I constantly rang the NHS with no luck but one day I came across a kind woman on the phone who took pity on me and sent me my mother's entire file going back years. It contained an alarming record of the various stupefying drugs she had been prescribed and reported that she had been unconscious for three days before coming into the hospital; she had been frozen and had needed three warmed blood transfusions. How was that possible? How could she freeze to death with Sam in the house? I suspected that he had drugged her and left her uncovered for three days and nights in front of an open window.

I knew that she would have never disinherited me or the children without being drugged up and coerced by Sam. I informed Sam of this new information and told him that his will was dodgy and that I believed him to have murdered my mother. I threatened to go to the police and he said, 'Oh please don't do that, if you keep quiet I'll go halves with you.' His panic was not the reaction of an innocent man so I called the cops immediately. He fled the country on a South Sea holiday but was ordered back for questioning, as were his two friends who had witnessed my mother's will.

The police told me that whilst these three men all sang the same tune – that she had voluntarily and in sound mind signed the will which Sam had drafted – there was nothing they could do. The only thing I could hope for was that they would fall out and betray Sam. Had she been buried there would certainly have been an exhumation for toxicology but her cremation ruled out that avenue of investigation. The police said that the solicitors were a disgrace and the first thing they should have told me when seeing her will was 'This is fishy, call the police' but despite my journalist friend from the *News of the World* putting pressure on them, they managed to bluff their way out of returning any of my money, justifying their bills by insisting 'they tried'. Eventually I signed a 'deed of variation' and Sam and I split my mother's assets. He gave me half her money and half her furniture and paintings and kept the house, on the pathetic grounds of his sentimental attachment to it, before promptly selling up. I had to cut my losses and cursed the day I had felt pity for that sad man in a hospital bed all those years ago. Throughout my life I have been a fool for picking up and helping lame ducks. Next time I shall walk by on the other side.

Sam died of drinking- and smoking-related diseases in March 2015, leaving all his possessions to a Mr Bell in Bristol, who had been a childhood friend. Following Sam's death, he kindly got in touch with me to ask if I wished to have my mother's photo albums back, which I was thrilled to receive. I gazed at the photos of her in her youth with an aching heart. And that was that. They were both dead and that chapter of my life was closed.

Graham also died in 2004. He was so hopelessly addicted to drink that he was unable to lead a normal life. He had a talent for art and spent his later days painting watercolours. That year both my kids were in Melbourne caring for him responsibly, as he was frequently hospitalised and sent into rehab. His alcoholic liver condition necessitated regular draining of the fluid build-up in his abdomen and Camilla said he often vomited blood. He was an endless problem and sad worry for them, as he lived all alone in our old house and they never knew what to expect.

I went to Melbourne to visit my children that August and remained there for three weeks, staying with Camilla. August was also Adam's birthday so it all worked out well, though the weather was drizzly and very cold. I cast my mind back to all those painful winters I had endured twenty years before and reassured myself that I would not be there for too long; Melbourne always made me feel physically ill. Graham wanted to see me but I could not face it. Even if we had conducted the meeting with civility, the memory of all the harm he had done me and the misery he had tyrannically inflicted was still sharp in my mind and I would have been ever fearful of him subjecting me to some form of mental battering. I was afraid I might cave in altogether if he said anything spiteful. I don't believe he was remorseful and I expected he would probe for a sign of weakness in me and exploit it with a sardonic comment. I had been married to the man and knew him well. It wasn't in his nature to be conciliatory and it wasn't in mine to be forgiving. One day my son took him out from the hospital and drove him to Camilla's house. I was told he was coming that afternoon so I went and sat in a coffee bar around the corner. I watched grimly as the car drove past with his head visible through the window.

Some years previous, I had received a letter from him, written on red paper for some reason, begging us to make up as he 'had always loved me' but I'd torn it up in disgust at his insincerity. Not long before this, just to show there's none so queer as folk, I also received two very sweet, considerate letters from Effie in which she wrote about her life and garden. To this day her motives for this puzzling change of heart elude me. Perhaps she realised that I was not all bad and had tried to do my best with her son, who she knew had a serious drinking problem. Or maybe she had caught wind of the success and prestige I was by now enjoying in England and thought to capitalise. Either way, Effie died in April 1998 after an unnecessary operation on her breast and strangely I was quite sorry for her and even sent flowers to her funeral. These days I generally think of her as a sad case, not truly malicious but simply ignorant and close-minded.

I left Melbourne on 23 August and while being driven to the airport I reflected on what a modern tale this was. I had met this devastatingly handsome man on holiday all those years ago, entered into a disastrous marriage and then my life had fast-forwarded to the moment when I was leaving on a jet plane with no word of farewell as he was lying on his deathbed.

He died on 28 August. When I heard the news I wept for about forty-five seconds and then composed myself. He had been a key player in my life but did not leave a single happy memory behind. That was his legacy. I remembered all the unceremonious, disgusting couplings which I had so dreaded. He had done his utmost to deprive me of my good name and my precious children. He had for years exerted his rights over my body, my money and never showed me a speck of kindness. After I left him, he had sought to tarnish my character further. I did not mourn his passing but I felt no reproach. What is done is done. His death certificate stated one cause of death as being thirty years of liver disease due to alcohol. When I read this I felt such rage that no Australian court had believed me about his drinking when I was fighting for custody of my children. The certificate also stated MRSA and peritonitis, the latter accounting for his grossly distended stomach, which burst a hole in the area of his belly button, being the point of least resistance, and rendered him susceptible to the hospital superbug, which affected him for one week. He had finally suffered 'massive hematemesis and melena' which lasted for one day. So he had died much the same way as Stefan had done.

Chapter 12

Throughout my years in the wilderness I was forever dreaming of the glamour, sophistication and nobility that characterised my teenage years in high society and ran in my blood. Despite all the horror of my days in Australia and the alcoholism and heartbreak that followed me back home, much like my father, I never stopped believing that God would take pity on me and I would be restored to my rightful place in the world. And so it came to pass that I did come to the attention of the royal family, I did get a house in Sloane Square and I did get horses and dogs, big ones and little ones, as if I had willed them into reality. These were the days of miracle and wonder.

Being a daredevil, Dick became a good horseman and we bought Hyde Park Stables in Bathurst Mews. He had played in Hyde Park as a child on the north side, as he lived in Paddington, and I had played in the park as a child too but I always went to the posh south side of Kensington Gardens. Ever since my childhood in Wetherby Mansions, I have been loopy about the place. At age seven I would regularly go fishing in the round pond; I had my fishing net with a long stick and my mother would give me a little jam jar with string around it to make a handle, so off I went to spend many happy hours catching sticklebacks. However, I didn't realise that you were supposed to keep them in pond water and when I put them into my aquarium filled with tap water they all died so I had to go and catch some more.

Riding around the park one day, it dawned on us that a huge section of Rotten Row had been destroyed between Marble Arch and Hyde Park Corner when Park Lane was widened in the 1950s.

Mother Anguish

We decided that its restoration was a project well worth undertaking and on proposing the idea were asked to do an interview for the local newspaper, in which I was correctly quoted as saying, 'It's nice to re-instate old traditions which were destroyed in the name of progress, i.e. a six-lane highway. It should never have been demolished in the first place. There has been a tremendous decline in horsey pursuits in the last century within the park and a new East Carriage Drive will encourage more horse people to use the park. This will benefit everyone by bringing a bit of countryside into the town.' As luck would have it HRH Prince Michael of Kent saw the article and his secretary contacted us to say that he would like a meeting as he felt the same way. After all, he was brought up in Kensington Palace and Hyde Park was as good as his own back garden.

Rotten Row has a fabulous history. The row was constructed in 1689 by the asthmatic William III as a carriage drive between Westminster and Kensington Palace. It was chosen to be the first lamp-lit road in London, as the area was a favourite spot for high-waymen. It then served as a hub of social activity for the next three hundred years, before gradually falling into disrepair. During the nineteenth century, which many referred to as the 'golden age of the horse', equestrian exercise was the most popular form of recrea-tion and a splendid marriage market, as anyone mounted on a fine animal was always shown to their best advantage. When Queen Victoria ascended the throne in 1837 the population of London was nearly 1.5 million, the capital throbbed with wealth and bustle and society revolved around the horse. An essential social ritual for all persons of fashion was a daily ride in Hyde Park.

Amongst the well-to-do, the daily gathering and meeting of friends in Rotten Row was a firmly established routine and it is difficult to believe today that regulations were set up to prevent dangerous overcrowding. It is hard to imagine in this day of car-dominated London, the amazing spectacle of up to one thousand horses and riders promenading up and down either side of the avenue of trees which divides Rotten Row, everyone vying for attention in their finest attire. Safety was of paramount consideration, especially after the death of Sir Robert Peel, founder of the Conservative Party and the police force. He suffered a fatal accident in the summer of 1850, having fallen from his horse and broken his collar bone, which pierced his jugular vein.

The grooms exercising their masters' horses were only permitted to do so before 7 a.m. These people were considered by some to be hooligans who rode recklessly and so were best gone by the time the gentry arrived. Frequent complaints were made about the 'galloping grooms' and it was arranged that police should supervise the exuberant antics. Early morning was also most popular for the 'liver shaking brigade', those high-living gentleman who, for the sake of their health and to counteract the ravages of dissipation due to the previous night's alcoholic excesses, would take their exercise, deeply breathing in the fresh morning air. No doubt their circulation and well-being benefited greatly, enabling them to recover enough to repeat the same enjoyment the following night.

The most popular time for ladies of fashion to see and be seen was between 11 a.m. and 1 p.m. Lady Augusta Fane reminisced in old age about her youth in the heyday of the park and the daily pageant of elegance; she recorded that the men wore dark cloth frock coats, very tight trousers, a collar and tie and a silk top hat, while ladies had a habit bodice buttoned to the neck, surrounded by a white collar, and white cuffs. A full long skirt, varnished boots and a silk top hat, similar to that of a gentleman, completed the costume.

All afternoon the show went on. William Makepeace Thackeray writes in his article on 'Military Snobs' that 'one is fully sure to see these raffish fellows lounging on horseback, about five o'clock, under the trees of the Serpentine. Watching the fashionable in the row afforded excellent entertainment for those who could not afford a horse but could lean on the elegant railings and bollards that lined the row.' Unfortunately all these elegant bollards were dug up and melted down for the war effort in 1941. In *The Times* newspaper, dated 2 December, it stated that three miles of railings were removed.

Oh, what a joy it was for me to now be involved in a dazzling project to restore these bollards. A scheme was founded, set into motion by the patronage of Prince Michael, whereby donors could sponsor them at a cost of £500 each and have their names inscribed at the top. Amongst the first patrons to hand over their cheque was the Duke of Wellington. Others included Barbara Cartland and even Andrew Parker Bowles bought one for his mum. The scheme to restore what was regarded as a vital part of Victorian London gained substantial support from such notables as the gloriously named Crown Equerry, Colonel Seymour Gilbart-Denham, who was responsible for the Royal Mews at Buckingham Palace during this time; ex-commanding officer Lieutenant Colonel Gordon Birdwood, adorably nicknamed 'Fluffy', a good, kind and funny man, loved by all who met him; and my very favourite soldier and Birdwood's successor, commanding officer Lieutenant Colonel Hamon Massey.

In September 1989, the Rotten Row Tercentenary Committee organised a cavalcade of a thousand horses and carriages, the largest procession of horses in London since the end of the Napoleonic Wars. It took place one sunny Sunday afternoon and little me was seated in the VIP section of the stand. At last I had come home and Melbourne was forgotten. Eat your heart out Graham and Effie, miracles do happen.

HRH Prince Michael opened the new East Carriage Ride bridleway in September and there was much rejoicing. Then Prince Michael unveiled the final phase: a magnificent set of gates would be built in honour of the Queen Mother, spanning the entrance to Hyde Park behind Aspley House. The Prince said, 'What was behind my idea of building the gates was the great affection for the Queen Mother, demonstrated last year nationwide on the occasion of her ninetieth birthday by people who wanted to show their gratitude.' HM Queen Mother had been the most popular Queen Consort of all time and I was honoured and thrilled beyond measure to be the general coordinator on this wonderful project.

I was therefore instrumental in fundraising for the Queen Mother's Gate, which was completed in 1993 to celebrate Her Majesty's ninety-third birthday and pay tribute to her lifetime of service to Britain and the Commonwealth. It was a mammoth and worthy task, especially given I had no previous experience of organising such a feat. I slaved away happily and wrote hundreds and hundreds of letters to all the rich people I could think of, saying that 'this gate will brighten the city in the same way that the Queen Mother has brightened our lives' and I thought to myself that if you are against this, you are a petty minded individual and you should be shot. Public-spirited individuals from all walks of life hastened to send in donations as soon as the scheme became known. One donation even came from an inmate of Wakefield Prison. I received an enormous amount of letters from organisations and firms with which the Queen Mother was involved and I answered them all.

For two years prior to the building of the gates, I also presided over monthly lunches and dinners held in the Officers' Mess of the Household Cavalry Barracks. I invited various captains of industry and commerce, who enthusiastically contributed to our fund. The dashing officers in full mess dress were also present to make nervous visitors welcome. They looked divinely decorative in their uniforms and ladies' hearts would flutter.

We did not want the gates to be a pastiche of the many Edwardian examples already dotted around Hyde Park, so instead the chosen design was light, feminine and fanciful. As a result, they are a symbol and celebration of modern gaiety and not dull or pompous in any way. The gates were made entirely by Giusseppe Lund and he oxidised the filigree metalwork so it became a riot of blue-tempered steel, green copper and titanium. The centrepiece of the lion and unicorn dancing around the tree of life was created by sculptor David Wynne.

Though many people who don't know what they are talking about pontificate about how much she hated them, Her Majesty the Queen Mother liked the gates very much. I was in charge throughout and in the spring of 1993 I took the architectural model to Clarence House for Her Majesty's approval and have numerous photos of her smiling happily and posing with it. Had the project been not to her liking, we would have abandoned it promptly and changed everything, as it was her birthday present. The only alteration she asked for was to have the lion and unicorn placed side by side, as originally David Wynne wanted the lion up in the tree.

Desmond Wilcox, the television producer, made a documentary about us and followed the progress of the gates' construction over a six-month period. This was broadcast on ITV on the night of the opening. Desmond was granted permission for admittance to Clarence House but it was made clear that he would film at a respectful distance and not speak, as the Queen Mother never gave interviews. We expected him to be on his best behaviour but were well aware of his mischievous and bombastic ways. On the day I dressed carefully and neatly as befits meeting the Queen Mother for the first time. I wore a navy suit with a deep white collar and set off for Clarence House at 10 a.m.

We were met at the door by William Tallon, a debonair, handsome man, resplendent in white tie and tails and bedecked with medals. He led up us up a huge hall to the Garden Room, where a beautiful but unfinished portrait of the Queen Mother as a young woman, painted by Augustus John, hangs over the fireplace. William had an instantly winning manner and a charming smile and he wasted no time in pressing a glass of champagne into my hand to put me at my ease. Her Majesty the Queen Mother entered the room a few minutes later dressed in royal blue and, I must admit, looked a bit wary upon seeing a full film crew in her house. Just previous to this Sir Alastair Aird, her divinely urbane and charming Private Secretary, who knew her well enough, voiced his concern that the Queen Mother might just walk in and say 'I don't like this' and walk out again. Sir Alistair had worked in the royal household since 1964 and was a stickler for elegant protocol and decorum. However, she did not and the atmosphere immediately became light-hearted and friendly. William stood unobtrusively as the Queen Mother asked me about my role in the project. Prince Michael mentioned that I was a vigorous fundraising letter-writer and, having made my lowest curtsy, I gibbered foolishly: 'I am the general dogsbody, Your Majesty. I am the envelope-stuffer, I do all the donkey work.' I caught William's eye and he winked.

Suddenly Desmond shocked us all by lurching into an interrogation of the Queen Mother while the cameras rolled. He thrust a microphone close to her face and we were horrified to hear him say, 'My goodness you have had a very long life, which has been the best bit?' She was taken aback but quickly retorted, 'There have been so many wonderful moments.' We were all frozen with panic and wanted to dive under the furniture in mortification. He then asked her what she would like to put in a time capsule of her life, suggesting a favourite salmon fly, the name of which he did not know. 'It's called a Blue Charm,' she said, 'and it sometimes works if you are lucky.' Desmond fawned obsequiously, 'Oh! Your Majesty, I think you are far too skilled to rely on luck,' and I saw William roll his eyes. 'I am not really a good fisherman but I do enjoy it,' she said. After each question we expected Desmond to quit while he was ahead and consider himself lucky he was not wrestled to the ground but there was no stopping him. His next question was, 'What advice would you give your grandchildren?' and she replied very firmly, 'Advice? I never give them advice except that they must always put their country first.' I watched helpless as her expression changed from that of good-humoured surprise to irritation, her eyes narrowing. Desmond continued grovelling: 'I am sure there is no doubt in anyone's mind that you have always done that, ma'am,' he said patronisingly. However, he had underestimated Her Majesty's experience in dealing with chatterboxes and although by now she certainly was not smiling anymore, went on asking questions until she gave her shoulders an elegant little shrug, tilted her head just so and turned her back frostily. Oh boy was she frosty. No wonder Hitler had called her 'The most dangerous woman in Europe'. She could look after herself and I had witnessed an unforgettable moment. I had seen Her Majesty's sweet side and also her tough side. Lunch was served and she left the room with Prince Michael.

'How could you do such a thing to an old woman, without any previous arrangement?' I railed at Desmond. 'You were supposed to keep quiet like a gentleman and speak when you were spoken to.' But the rascal was delighted with himself and flippantly replied he liked taking people unawares and asking awkward questions as it 'encouraged spontaneity'. And besides, he said, he would never get such a brilliant opportunity again and he wasn't going to waste it. Even so, I was pretty cross and told him that if someone ambushed my old granny like that, I would punch their lights out.

The following day William invited me for tea at his home, Gate Lodge, a miniature flat-roofed bungalow that stood at the entrance to Clarence House. And for the next few years we became good friends and he amused me with endless funny stories.

He told me that the Queen Mother had been very distressed at being trapped by Desmond and wished she had had some warning so she could have prepared what to say. William consequently had a row with Sir Alastair Aird over the fact that he ought to have briefed Desmond beforehand. William was too flamboyant and gay and Sir Alastair thought he was over-familiar with the Queen Mother, so consequently William and Sir Alastair never got on. All that being said, the documentary shown on ITV was very good and the fuss died down.

Basia Briggs

The months leading up to the opening ceremony were fraught with mountains of paperwork and the phone constantly rang with people begging for invitations. All this flurry of activity had a fantastic effect on me; my mood bubbled and I threw aside all feelings of tension. I was in sole charge of the guest list; I would answer to no one and not give in to bullies. I had to explain that I was only inviting those who had donated £5,000 or more but I was approached by an endless stream of opportunists who did their best to befriend me under the guise of friendship and I confess I made some ghastly contacts. My only excuse was that I was inexperienced and guilty of the giddy innocence of youth. I even had some people complaining that I shouldn't be in such an important position as 'I wasn't even English'. But I had had in my life enough taunts of racism; as with many other Polish persons of consequence, I was always made to feel like the underdog but as a people it has kept us sharp and chirpy and hungry for victory with unlimited enthusiasm in love and war. I like winning in life and I like winning by a lot and then I was on the crest of a wave; I was unassailable and would let nothing daunt me.

We had a very humorous exchange of correspondence with the Worshipful Company of Blacksmiths, a livery company dating back to the fourteenth century. They originally submitted a design which was rejected. Stung that their trade should produce such a well-publicised example of ironmongery without any reference to them, the Worshipfuls continued to pester me, criticising the design for being 'airy-fairy' and telling me that the gates would 'not be as long-lasting as the Queen Mother' as the public would pull bits off them. Undeterred by their rejection and my uninterested response to their complaints, the Blacksmiths then asked for an invitation to the opening ceremony, so we replied that there was 'a lack of space'. To this they responded with a vitriolic letter, saying that 'true blacksmiths of this country will be pleased that the Worshipful Company of Blacksmiths is not associated with the Gate'. Having hammered their point home, they retired hurt.

The gate was opened on 6 July 1993. It was on time, on budget and the sun shone. Before the audience proceeded to take their seats, it was the duty of Lieutenant Colonel Hamon Massey and I to shake hands with all 900 of the invited guests at the entrance but I was forced to give up and leave the mighty soldier to it after about 400 as some squeezed so hard that that my rings caused me not inconsiderable pain. Her Majesty the Queen performed the opening ceremony in front of the invitees, all seated in a large stand, and on the opposite side of the row was the royal stand where I sat; at the very front along with the Queen, the Queen Mother, Prince and Princess Michael of Kent and the Lord Lieutenant of London. I have to admit that I never invited my mother as I was mortified at the thought of her saying something about my father's willy in this exalted company. There were thousands of other spectators lining the streets and coachloads of little children waving flags, not to mention the huge gathered throng of officials, television men and security policemen. I was a thousand light years away from those desolate and despairing days in Melbourne which had threatened to destroy me. The band of the Household Cavalry, with their trumpets and all their clamouring and clanking splendour, played rousing marches and the worst thing that happened was that a group of militant lesbians with ladders had managed to climb into Buckingham Palace gardens that morning. I remember the Queen saying with a wry smile, 'Why me?'

The newspapers at the time were full of hilarious criticism, which we took in good humour even though some of the articles were downright beastly. Lord St John of Fawsley was one of the more complimentary commentators and described them as 'full of joy, strength and courage like the great personage in whose honour they have been created'. However, Nick Tite, editor of the *RA Magazine*, said that 'They look like three-dimensional knitting,' and Brian Sewell remarked that they were 'more suitable for a pantomime finale'. Lord Rogers, director general of the Royal Institute of Architects, said, 'This is all romantic candyfloss and there is more than a hint of one of her hats in the design,' and other people said much worse but twenty years have passed and, although controversial, they are nevertheless a resounding success and appear much loved.

The day after the successful opening, having worked on the project for three years, I had no reason to get up in the morning. But a phone call from HRH Prince Michael soon perked me up. The following Sunday HRH Prince Michael took us to the Grand Prix, my very first time in a helicopter. I wore flowing cream silk and a cream hat. We took off from Battersea heliport at 9 a.m. and I sat with Lord Renwick, who was splendid company and soothed my nerves. Helicopters are the only way to travel; they feel a little odd as they never appear to be moving forwards but we were in Northampton in no time after gazing from above at the traffic jams on the motorway. We arrived at Silverstone at 9:40 a.m. and were ushered into the main observation tower; needless to say we had the best view. While enjoying lunch and watching the race from our spectacular vantage point, I met King Hussein of Jordan and also little Prince Harry, who would have been about ten. He kept saying excitedly, 'Look at Damon, look at Damon,' referring to Damon Hill, as the cars roared around.

On another occasion Prince Michael took me to the London to Brighton rally, an event I was very much looking forward to as I've always had a passion for vintage cars. I was told to wrap up warm but nothing prepared me for the wind chill factor during the four-hour open-top drive to Brighton in his 1901 Mors without a windscreen. On the day I got up at 3:30 a.m. to pretty myself up and then proceeded to layer on seven jumpers, thinking that this surely would be enough; I must warn people, however, it is not. I was to later learn that one absolutely must wear leather. At 5 a.m.

Mother Anguish

I went to Kensington Palace to meet the Prince and we then had a hearty breakfast, the full English with fried bread. Approaching the South Carriage Ride to muster with other participating vehicles was a surreal experience. Dawn was breaking and through the mist all manner of cars were converging; every colour, shape and size had its representative. They all lined up in a row and by then it was light so we all walked the length to observe the glorious spectacle of this multitude of old automobiles covered in shiny knobs and hooters. We managed the drive without breaking down. HRH Prince Michael, who is the most reserved royal with the most regal bearing, turns into a complete hooligan once behind the wheel of a vintage car and we enjoyed being cheered on by about million people en route. We arrived in Brighton in glorious sunshine; the sea was sparkling, the band played and we all had a celebratory lunch.

The following year, Prince Michael took me again but this time I had learnt my lesson and was determined not to freeze. Even the royal policeman last time had jokingly said to me, 'Have you seen your face Basia?' so I had looked in the mirror and was horror-struck to see myself totally mottled with purple and sporting a bright blue nose and dead-looking lilac lips. This time, I put on thermal underwear, a thermal vest and on top of that a black dustbin liner, in which I had cut a hole for my head and two on either side for my arms. Above this, I wore two more jumpers, another plastic bin liner and then a final jumper to look good for the photographers. I rustled a bit but I was as warm as toast.

Back in London I saw a lot of William Tallon and became a frequent visitor to Gate Lodge. I greatly enjoyed his flamboyant and legendary hospitability; he entertained the more interesting and cultured people from show business and the arts world in his mini palace. His taste was exquisite yet homely; the Queen Mother had given him beautiful pictures and antique furniture and every surface of every table was laden with precious objects, including gold and silver boxes he had received as presents from Royalty, all bearing inscribed messages of thanks for his service. All around the room in large silver frames there were many personally signed photographs of members of the royal family, including the Duke and Duchess of Windsor. Guests had to sit two to a chair or on the floor, as his cottage was so tiny.

William also often called at my house and each time told me, amongst much giggling, of how as a teenager he had lost his virginity at the corner house of my street, which had been notorious male brothel. However, I never asked him for the details.

He was so joyful during the 1990s. He loved his life; he loved his partner Reg Wilcock, another jovial butler with a wonderful laugh and soothing personality; and he loved the Queen Mother from the first day he met her. She lifted the spirits of all those with whom she came into contact and it is no wonder she was so incredibly popular. William recalled that once, when he was seventeen and working in Buckingham Palace, he innocently gave her a postal order for seven shillings and sixpence as a gift voucher for her birthday; a substantial chunk of his wage. He said he was reprimanded severely for this; 'But I just loved her so much,' he told me. He had started working for the royal family in 1951 as a bootblack and junior steward. As the years passed he became absorbed into the sleek world of life at court. He did not have to exert himself to achieve power. Such was his engaging and sunny disposition and his natural wit and efficiency, that his company became indispensable in whatever situation as he always provided the jokes and good humour.

As well as keeping each other smiling, they also had many serious talks and William recounted that when she was seventy-five, the Queen Mother advised him not to trust anyone, ever. The Queen Mother's intense and staunch affection for him was undoubted and his influence over her provoked much resentment from the other staff. He was her most trusted servant, her confidante, her court jester and sometimes her advisor and spy. There was a passionate sincerity in their fondness for one another and the bond was unbreakable despite countless plots by jealous officials. William reigned supreme at Clarence House and he embraced the spectacular good fortune life had bestowed on him.

The Queen Mother entertained a great deal and for William it was always 'show time'. Fascinating guests would be invited for lunch and dinner and she thrived on lively conversation and plenty of gossip and gaiety. Occasionally guests made the mistake of asking her how old her dogs were and this displeased her. 'Oh God, are we to be reduced to talking about dogs' ages now,' she once said. To loosen up nervous visitors, William would often slip some vodka into the tea, a trick of his well known to the Queen Mother but one which was never met with any disapproval. People on their best behaviour would suddenly become delightfully tipsy and jocular without the foggiest notion that they had been spiked. There was a documentary made about William called *Backstairs Billy* and the great royal pundit Hugo Vickers was quoted as saying, 'One man had to be more or less carried out because he hadn't realised that these nice drinks he was having were pretty potent stuff.'

William was also very fond of Diana, who spent her last night as a bride-to-be at Clarence House. Contrary to reports that she rode a bicycle around the gardens yelling, 'I am going to marry the Prince of Wales in the morning', she actually rode the bicycle in the house, round and round William's office, which was a very large room. It was a hot summer's night and he recalled that she went to bed exhilarated before her wedding. She did not like duvets, preferring sheets and to be well tucked in, like a little girl.

Once William told me that he and Mr Baker, another butler, had been drinking pink gin all afternoon before the Queen was due to come to tea. The Queen's band of killer corgis had recently had a bloodthirsty fight and one, called Heather, had come out of it rather badly. She had had to have a leg amputated and also lost both her ears. When Her Majesty arrived, she brought Heather with her but Mr Baker did not know the story and when he saw the dog he went rushing back to William, saying, 'No more gin, I have just seen a three-legged dog with no ears!'

One summer's day I called in on William after a Buckingham Palace garden party to show him my new hat. The Mall was congested with traffic and afterwards I had trouble crossing the road. William was so conscious of his personal grandeur and confident in his authority whilst in uniform, that he just held my hand and waded straight into the river of cars with arms outstretched. All the vehicles stopped for him without protest. It was like Moses parting the waves.

The Queen Mother and everyone else adored Reg Wilcock; the Page of the Presence and William's long-term lover, who had started working at Clarence House in 1957. When he died in August 2000 Prince Charles told William that 'Granny will never get over this' and that the Queen Mother herself had said there would never be so much laughter in any of her houses again now that he was gone. Reg had a magnificent funeral, for which William chose the music; he even asked if the National Anthem could be played and the Queen agreed, 'but only the one verse.'

Following Reg's death I saw more and more of William. He would ring me in a deep depression, asking me to come over and see him. One time, William asked me to keep him company, as he was lonely and had to wait for the plumber to come and fix his lavatory. When I arrived William had prepared his favourite tuna fish and cucumber sandwiches and a plate full of devilled eggs and we drank champagne. Later we were joined by the actor Leonard Whiting, who had played the lead in Franco Zeffirelli's *Romeo and Juliet*, and whose buttocks, William had informed me, were the most beautiful in Europe. A young blond plumber came and unblocked the loo and William offered him champagne and enquired about his life and where he was from. 'Essex,' said the plumber. 'And where in Essex?' queried William. 'Hornchurch,' came the answer and then William exclaimed with enthusiasm, 'Oh, Hornchurch, of course!' 'Do you know Hornchurch?' asked the plumber brightly, to which William replied vehemently, 'Of course I don't!' and we all laughed. I guessed that William fancied the plumber but he escaped. After the plumber left, we all went to a dinner party in Highgate. Leonard was there with another man who was a defrocked priest. They were constantly bandying sexual innuendoes between them and making humorous banter and I cringed and was rather embarrassed. Once Leonard said, 'I bent over backwards to help you' and William laughingly joked, 'I wish you would bend over forwards.'

When the Queen Mother died on 30 March 2002, William was very distressed by the fact that he was not informed by any palace officials, despite having been her loyal servant for fifty-one years. Just one and a half years had separated the deaths of Reg and the Queen Mother and William was distraught and got terribly drunk. Shortly after the funeral he chopped up his old uniform. He was ordered to vacate his beloved Gate Lodge, where he had lived for so long, and he was heartbroken. He felt wretched and bewildered to be so punished, having done nothing blameworthy, but he said his foes were united in a hatred of him based on sheer jealousy.

Often in his last years William and I would go the Doghouse, a large pub in Kennington Road near his home. He possessed a genius for creating rapport with complete strangers, however disreputable, enquiring about their lives and sometimes, in moments of insane recklessness, inviting them home for a drink, where I worried they might steal or do him harm. Dick was also alarmed and disapproving. He was fond of William but thought he was a bad influence on me and he was always anxious about me getting a taxi home on my own late at night. One night William and I were seated at the bar, very jolly, when suddenly I saw my husband's furious face at the side window, his nose pressed against the pane. We pointed at him, giggling uncontrollably, but sobered up quickly when he stormed the pub. He seized William by the hand, pulling him off his stool and forcibly led us out, yelling all the while that we were a drunken disgrace. Some customers booed in sympathy as we were dragged along like two naughty children. William and I were still giggling as we walked arm-in-arm, zigzagging along the pavement, while my husband drove the five hundred yards to William's home along the kerb next to us.

Shortly after, William and I went to the designer Nicky Haslam's book launch across the road from where I live. The glamour of the guest list and the flowing champagne made me tipsy and I was in no state to drive William home. It worried me to think of him on the night bus but my friend assured me she would take him home safely. Instead, she put him into a taxi and he stopped at the Dog-house and continued drinking. Staggering home, he fell over and was photographed by paparazzi, the pictures causing a sensation over the next few days. Although humiliated, William wanted us to go to San Lorenzo for lunch the Saturday after and be photographed sober. But while William's enemies gloated, Prince Charles was swift with kind-heartedness and invited William up to Balmoral for a few days. William was devoted to the Prince of Wales as he considered himself to be something of a father figure to him, having cared for the Prince as a child whenever the Queen was away.

In the summer of 2006, William's health deteriorated dreadfully. He lost four stone in weight and was hospitalised at St Mary's, Paddington. He was yellow was jaundice and his beautiful, thick hair was now sparse and wispy. When I visited him he said he just wanted to die and he told me he had his funeral all prepared. Prince Charles also visited him, which was a pleasant shock for the hospital staff.

In November 2007, two weeks before he died, we caught a bus from Sloane Square to Piccadilly and walked up to Burlington Arcade where he brought me some chocolate, once more in high spirits like old times. His sunny nature had triumphed and I was so glad. His zest for life was greater that his need for death. He was dressed in bright green corduroy trousers, a pale blue and bright purple striped jumper, a brown checked tweed jacket and a bright red scarf and that is how I shall remember him. I never saw him again. God rest his gallant old soul.

He told many more stories which I don't care to mention out of tact and consideration for the royal family. Whenever I get pumped by the press, I retreat behind a veil of discretion and always say, 'Sorry gentlemen, I can't say another word. State secret.' However, my other favourite shaggy dog story, which is not too controversial, involved the Prince of Wales, who had two Jack Russells named Tigger and Pooh. One day Tigger entered the kitchen of Highgrove, disturbing the cook, who didn't like dogs on his territory. So to teach poor Tigger a lesson, he scooped him up and put him into the still-warm oven. Unfortunately for the kitchen staff, Prince Charles walked in from the garden, which was the last thing they were expecting, and asked, 'Has anyone seen Tigger?' No one managed to reply sensibly, except to say that they thought he had gone this or that way away from the kitchen. Prince Charles stayed chatting a while, all the time not knowing that his dog was right under his nose locked in an oven. The moment he left, they removed poor, panting Tigger and chucked him through another doorway into the corridor, before soon afterwards hearing the Prince of Wales say, 'Hello Tigger, you look hot!'

Since my return to Sloane Square and fashionable society, my days have been filled with much glamour and delight. I seem to be invited everywhere that matters and am regularly surrounded by university-educated people of high rank and position who stimulate my mind and sense of humour. It is a far cry indeed from my days of drudgery in the cultural wasteland of the outer-Melbourne suburban bush. However, the thing I am most thankful for is not the royal patronage, the inspiring people I surround myself with, nor my beautiful home in its idyllic surroundings but the freedom.

Yes it is the freedom; a freedom that I glory in each and every day and one that fills me with such a sense of wonder. After the tyranny of the nuns at La Sagesse and my other boarding schools and my days of servitude at the hands of Graham, just to know that I can get up at whatever time I like and be answerable to no one gives me such joy. I will never again let anyone order me about or give any-one rights over my time, my body and my money. I come and go as I please and see whoever I desire, spend what I want, go to bed when I choose and eat as often as I please, without Graham there to castigate me for 'stuffing my face' again. I do no housework, although occasionally on a sunny day I take pleasure in polishing my furniture and seeing everything gleam around me.

Epilogue

Looking back, I am not a prisoner of the past because of my time in Australia; it was a lesson not a life sentence. The vicissitudes of my youth have, thank God, been somewhat left behind me on the wayside and though the diverging paths of life hold infinite possibilities, mine have led me to many wonderful opportunities and experiences. Who knows the pitfalls of other less circuitous routes? Since my return from Antipodean exile, I have often lived a life most would dream of and for that I can at least be grateful.

However, the fact is that whilst I have made a 'success' of my life, it has come at a terrible cost. Dick and I have made a rewarding partnership of a marriage but it has nevertheless caused untold misery and much painful disturbance to my children, who spent their entire childhood traumatised by the consequences of me leaving their father; the court cases, the constant tearful goodbyes at airports and our prolonged separations in their tender years have all taken their toll. I had been a mumsy full-time parent and their lives had been sunny and full of joy and happiness before I destroyed that stability they cherished; a stability I feel such remorse for taking away, since I lacked it too and know of the terrible consequences suffered in its absence. They still reproach me for the catastrophic upheaval of their lives and my daughter Camilla, for instance, refuses to ever come to London as she doesn't like Dick, a legacy of his drunken years early on in our marriage.

I feel anguish for my mother's demise and always will until the day I die. As could be expected, she was not one to take her advancing years alongside my rise in society with any good grace and she did her best to make life difficult for me and exhaust my once abundant compassion until the very last. But it was still my duty to care for her. As Daniel Topolski, always one for an astute observation of her character, once said to me, 'She just never grew up,' and that about sums it up. She couldn't help being the way she was. Though jaded, the love for the glamorous, enchanting and frightfully silly woman observed through childhood eyes remains and I am haunted with eternal shame that I was not keeping a closer eye on her before she died. To this day Sam Parker is the only person I regret helping. I was too short-sighted to see his cruel and manipulative intentions and that mistake, along with my failure to put an end to his criminal neglect, has come at an unbearably heavy cost. But she and Sam are both dead now and what's done is done; tracing the diverging paths of the past offers no solution. I sincerely hope she met Mr Henryk and Mr Kieconski in heaven.

Acknowledgements

I would like to express my overwhelming and boundless gratitude to Naim Attallah for suggesting the book in the first place and thereafter coaxing, cajoling, sweetly nagging and forcing me to put aside my shame and embarrassment, and put pen to paper. I am conscious of the enormity of my debt to him for giving me a purpose and scooping me up at the most terrible and sad time of my life. His kindness and concern for my welfare and happiness is not something I have oft encountered; a wonderful man and he has my undying love and affection. My eternal thanks goes to Peter Jacobs, to whom I am beholden immeasurably for not only refining the text but for his extraordinary perception, clarity of mind, insight and patience which have navigated me with assurance through all the complexities and challenges faced by a debut author. I would like to thank all at Quartet Books: James Pulford for being charmingly stern with calm authority and Grace Pilkington for being unfailingly cheerful, helpful and generous. Finally I want to pay tribute to my husband Richard Briggs for allowing me to write truthfully about his background and behaviour (plenty more where that came from but that's another story); a brave decision on his part.